At Sylvan, we believe that a lifelong love of learning begins at an early age, and we are glad you have chosen our resources to help your children experience the joy of mathematics as they build critical reasoning skills. We know that the time you spend with your children reinforcing the lessons learned in school will contribute to their love of learning.

Success in math requires more than just memorizing basic facts and algorithms; it also requires children to make sense of size, shape, and numbers as they appear in the world. Children who can connect their understanding of math to the world around them will be ready for the challenges of mathematics as they advance to more complex topics.

We use a research-based, step-by-step process in teaching math at Sylvan that includes thought-provoking math problems and activities. As students increase their success as problem solvers, they become more confident. With increasing confidence, students build even more success. The design of the Sylvan workbooks will help you to help your children build the skills and confidence that will contribute to success in school.

We're excited to partner with you to support the development of a confident, well-prepared, independent learner!

The Sylvan Team

1st Grade
Basic Math Success
Workbook

Published in the United States by Random House, Inc., New York, and in Canada by Random House of Canada Limited, Toronto.

www.sylvanlearning.com

Created by Smarterville Productions LLC
Producer & Editorial Direction: The Linguistic Edge
Producer: TJ Trochlil McGreevy
Writer: Amy Kraft
Cover and Interior Illustrations: Shawn Finley and Duendes del Sur
Layout and Art Direction: SunDried Penguin
Director of Product Development: Russell Ginns

First Edition

ISBN: 978-0-375-43034-3

Library of Congress Cataloging-in-Publication Data available upon request.

This book is available at special discounts for bulk purchases for sales promotions or premiums. For more information, write to Special Markets/Premium Sales, 1745 Broadway, MD 6-2, New York, New York 10019 or e-mail specialmarkets@randomhouse.com.

PRINTED IN CHINA

10 9 8 7

Contents

Numbers & Operations to 10

1. **Counting to 10** — 2
2. **Adding Sums to 10** — 6
3. **Subtracting Differences from 10** — 12
   Review — 18

Numbers & Operations to 20

4. **Counting to 20** — 22
5. **Adding Sums to 20** — 26
6. **Subtracting Differences from 20** — 32
   Review — 38

Place Value & Number Sense

7. **Counting to 100** — 42
8. **Ones, Tens & Hundreds** — 48
9. **Number Lines & Patterns** — 54
10. **Comparing Numbers** — 58
    Review — 62

Geometry

11. **Drawing & Comparing Shapes** — 66
12. **Transforming Shapes** — 72
13. **Symmetry** — 76
    Review — 80

Measurement

14. **Nonstandard Units** — 84
15. **Inches & Centimeters** — 88
16. **Approximation & Estimation** — 92
    Review — 96

Time

17. **Telling Time in Hours** — 98
18. **Telling Time in Half Hours** — 102
    Review — 106

Money

19. **Coin Values** — 108
20. **Using Coins** — 112
    Review — 116
    Answers — 118

Practice the Numbers

COUNT the cubes. Then TRACE each number and word.

 ――1―― ――one――

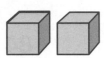 ――2―― ――two――

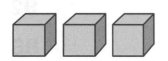 ――3―― ―three―

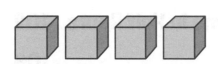 ――4―― ――four――

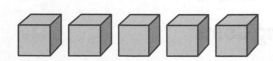 ――5―― ――five――

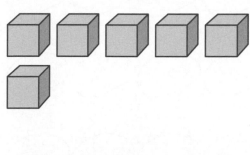

——— 6 ———   ——— six ———

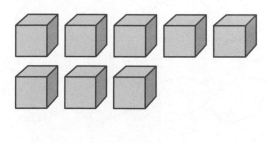

——— 7 ———   ——— seven ———

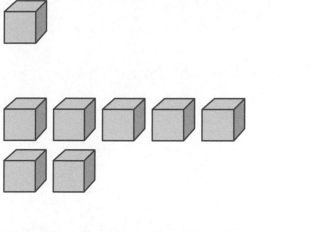

——— 8 ———   ——— eight ———

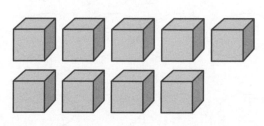

——— 9 ———   ——— nine ———

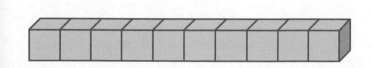

——— 10 ———   ——— ten ———

Counting to 10

Color Groups

LOOK at each number. COLOR the correct number of jellybeans to match the number.

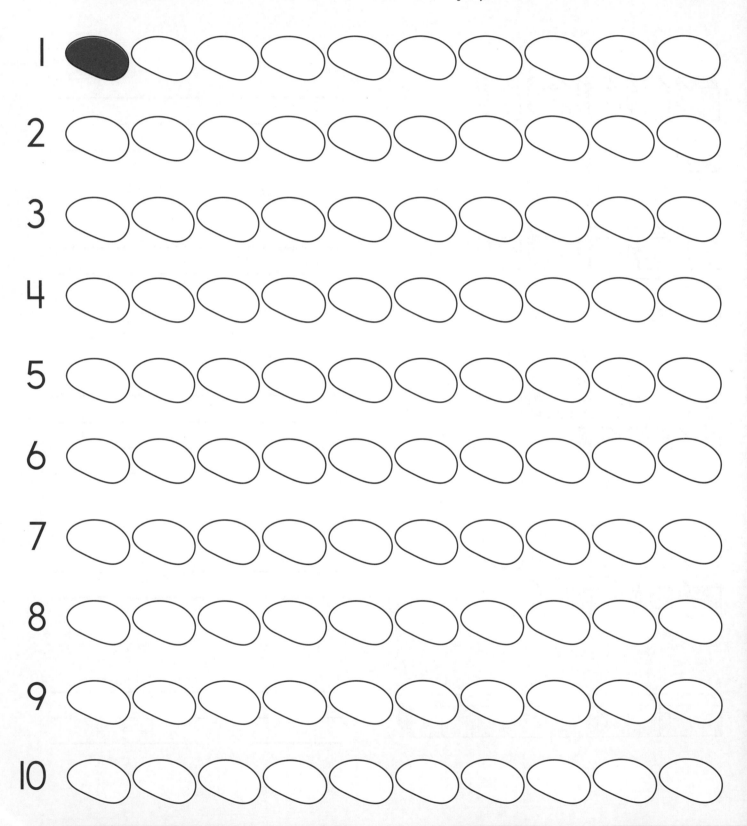

Match Up

DRAW lines to connect the numbers and pictures that go together.

7

10

9

6

4

3

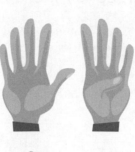

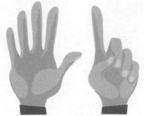

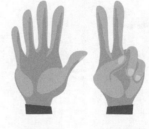

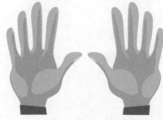

Picture It

WRITE the number of pieces of candy you see in each jar. ADD the two numbers, and WRITE how much candy there is in both jars.

1.

$$5 + 1 = 6$$

2.

$$\square + \square = \square$$

3.

$$\square + \square = \square$$

4.

$$\square + \square = \square$$

5.

$$\square + \square = \square$$

6.

$$\square + \square = \square$$

Picture It

WRITE the number of dots you see. ADD the two numbers, and WRITE the number of dots there are on each domino.

1.  + $\begin{array}{r} 2 \\ 3 \\ \hline 5 \end{array}$

2.  +

3. 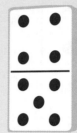 +

4. 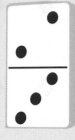 +

5.  +

6.  +

7.  +

8.  +

9.  +

Card Tricks

DRAW a line to connect each card at the bottom to the place where it belongs.

+ 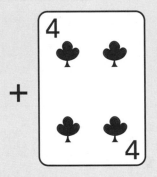 + 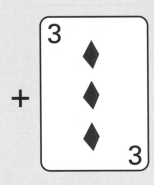 +  +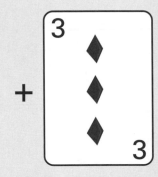

Marble Mania

WRITE the number of marbles you see. ADD the two numbers, and WRITE the total number of marbles.

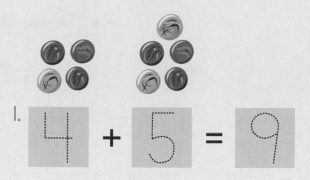

1. 4 + 5 = 9

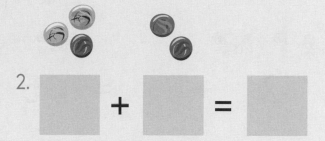

2. ___ + ___ = ___

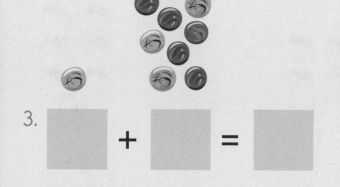

3. ___ + ___ = ___

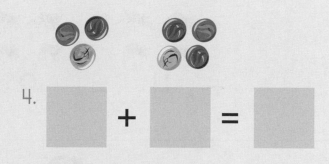

4. ___ + ___ = ___

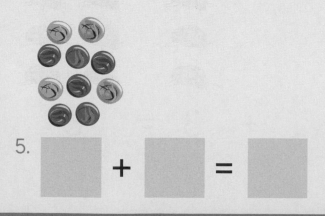

5. ___ + ___ = ___

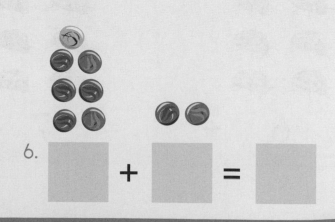

6. ___ + ___ = ___

Bug Collection

WRITE the missing number.

HINT: Count the bugs to help you.

1.

2 + ☐ = 5

2.

☐ + 1 = 8

3.

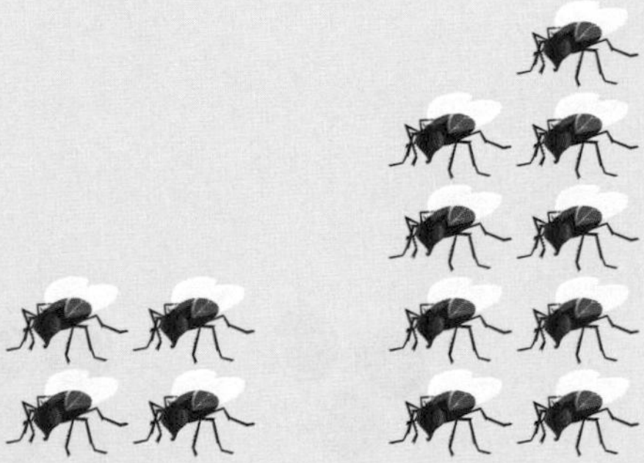

☐ + 4 = 9

4.

4 + ☐ = 10

5.

6 + ☐ = 7

6.

☐ + 3 = 6

2

It All Adds Up

WRITE each sum.

1.
$$\begin{array}{r} 7 \\ + 2 \\ \hline \end{array}$$

2.
$$\begin{array}{r} 3 \\ + 5 \\ \hline \end{array}$$

3.
$$\begin{array}{r} 4 \\ + 1 \\ \hline \end{array}$$

4.
$$\begin{array}{r} 6 \\ + 2 \\ \hline \end{array}$$

5.
$$\begin{array}{r} 10 \\ + 0 \\ \hline \end{array}$$

6.
$$\begin{array}{r} 2 \\ + 1 \\ \hline \end{array}$$

7.
$$\begin{array}{r} 7 \\ + 3 \\ \hline \end{array}$$

8.
$$\begin{array}{r} 5 \\ + 4 \\ \hline \end{array}$$

9.
$$\begin{array}{r} 1 \\ + 9 \\ \hline \end{array}$$

10.
$$\begin{array}{r} 5 \\ + 2 \\ \hline \end{array}$$

11.
$$\begin{array}{r} 8 \\ + 1 \\ \hline \end{array}$$

12.
$$\begin{array}{r} 0 \\ + 7 \\ \hline \end{array}$$

13.
$$\begin{array}{r} 2 \\ + 2 \\ \hline \end{array}$$

14.
$$\begin{array}{r} 4 \\ + 3 \\ \hline \end{array}$$

15.
$$\begin{array}{r} 6 \\ + 1 \\ \hline \end{array}$$

16.
$$\begin{array}{r} 4 \\ + 4 \\ \hline \end{array}$$

Subtracting Differences from 10

The Cupcake Eater

How many cupcakes are left on the plate after the Cupcake Eater eats some? WRITE the answer.

HINT: Cross off the number of eaten cupcakes, and count how many are left.

1.  $4 - 1 = $ 3

cupcakes   eaten

2.  $5 - 3 = $

3.  $7 - 2 = $

4.  $8 - 6 = $

Cracking Eggs

DRAW cracks on the eggs, and COUNT how many eggs are left. WRITE the number.

1.
$$
\begin{array}{r}
5 \text{ eggs} \\
- 2 \text{ cracked eggs} \\
\hline
3
\end{array}
$$

2.
$$
\begin{array}{r}
8 \\
- 4 \\
\hline
\end{array}
$$

3.
$$
\begin{array}{r}
7 \\
- 1 \\
\hline
\end{array}
$$

4.
$$
\begin{array}{r}
9 \\
- 4 \\
\hline
\end{array}
$$

5.
$$
\begin{array}{r}
3 \\
- 1 \\
\hline
\end{array}
$$

6.
$$
\begin{array}{r}
10 \\
- 5 \\
\hline
\end{array}
$$

13

Subtracting Differences from 10

Card Tricks

DRAW a line to connect each card at the bottom to the place where it belongs.

Bowled Over

Each row shows how many pins were standing at the start and end of a bowling turn. WRITE the number of pins that were knocked over.

1. $10 - \boxed{} = 5$

2. $10 - \boxed{} = 8$

3. $8 - \boxed{} = 4$

4. $4 - \boxed{} = 1$

5. $6 - \boxed{} = 2$

6. $7 - \boxed{} = 3$

Subtracting Differences from 10

What's the Difference?

WRITE each difference.

1.
$$8 - 2 = \square$$

2.
$$9 - 7 = \square$$

3.
$$4 - 3 = \square$$

4.
$$5 - 1 = \square$$

5.
$$10 - 9 = \square$$

6.
$$6 - 4 = \square$$

7.
$$1 - 0 = \square$$

8.
$$7 - 2 = \square$$

9.
$$3 - 1 = \square$$

10.
$$5 - 5 = \square$$

11.
$$9 - 3 = \square$$

12.
$$10 - 7 = \square$$

13.
$$4 - 0 = \square$$

14.
$$9 - 8 = \square$$

15.
$$3 - 2 = \square$$

16.
$$8 - 5 = \square$$

Fact Finder

COMPLETE each fact family. *Example:* 2 + 3 = 5 5 – 2 = 3
3 + 2 = 5 5 – 3 = 2

1. 4 + 5 = 9

☐ + ☐ = ☐
☐ – ☐ = ☐
☐ – ☐ = ☐

2. 6 + 2 = 8

☐ + ☐ = ☐
☐ – ☐ = ☐
☐ – ☐ = ☐

3. 2 + 1 = 3

☐ + ☐ = ☐
☐ – ☐ = ☐
☐ – ☐ = ☐

4. 3 + 4 = 7

☐ + ☐ = ☐
☐ – ☐ = ☐
☐ – ☐ = ☐

5. 1 + 5 = 6

☐ + ☐ = ☐
☐ – ☐ = ☐
☐ – ☐ = ☐

6. 7 + 3 = 10

☐ + ☐ = ☐
☐ – ☐ = ☐
☐ – ☐ = ☐

Beetlemania

COUNT the beetles. Then WRITE the number of beetles.

1. 3

2.

3.

4.

5.

6.

7.

8.

9.

Unit Rewind

WRITE each sum or difference.

1.
$$\begin{array}{r} 5 \\ + 4 \\ \hline \end{array}$$

2.
$$\begin{array}{r} 6 \\ + 1 \\ \hline \end{array}$$

3.
$$\begin{array}{r} 3 \\ + 2 \\ \hline \end{array}$$

4.
$$\begin{array}{r} 1 \\ + 9 \\ \hline \end{array}$$

5.
$$\begin{array}{r} 10 \\ + 0 \\ \hline \end{array}$$

6.
$$\begin{array}{r} 2 \\ + 7 \\ \hline \end{array}$$

7.
$$\begin{array}{r} 4 \\ + 4 \\ \hline \end{array}$$

8.
$$\begin{array}{r} 0 \\ + 5 \\ \hline \end{array}$$

9.
$$\begin{array}{r} 8 \\ - 5 \\ \hline \end{array}$$

10.
$$\begin{array}{r} 3 \\ - 3 \\ \hline \end{array}$$

11.
$$\begin{array}{r} 1 \\ - 0 \\ \hline \end{array}$$

12.
$$\begin{array}{r} 9 \\ - 7 \\ \hline \end{array}$$

13.
$$\begin{array}{r} 6 \\ - 4 \\ \hline \end{array}$$

14.
$$\begin{array}{r} 10 \\ - 5 \\ \hline \end{array}$$

15.
$$\begin{array}{r} 7 \\ - 1 \\ \hline \end{array}$$

16.
$$\begin{array}{r} 5 \\ - 4 \\ \hline \end{array}$$

Review

Unit Rewind

WRITE the missing number in each problem.

1. $7 + \boxed{} = 9$

2. $+ 5 = 6$

3. $+ 4 = 7$

4. $2 + \boxed{} = 10$

5. $3 + \boxed{} = 8$

6. $+ 2 = 4$

7. $\boxed{} - 1 = 9$

8. $10 - \boxed{} = 2$

9. $8 - \boxed{} = 2$

10. $- 2 = 5$

11. $\boxed{} - 6 = 3$

12. $4 - \boxed{} = 1$

Fact Finder

COMPLETE each fact family.

1. 4 + 1 = 5

☐ + ☐ = ☐

☐ − ☐ = ☐

☐ − ☐ = ☐

2. 7 + 2 = 9

☐ + ☐ = ☐

☐ − ☐ = ☐

☐ − ☐ = ☐

3. 6 + 4 = 10

☐ + ☐ = ☐

☐ − ☐ = ☐

☐ − ☐ = ☐

4. 5 + 3 = 8

☐ + ☐ = ☐

☐ − ☐ = ☐

☐ − ☐ = ☐

5. 4 + 2 = 6

☐ + ☐ = ☐

☐ − ☐ = ☐

☐ − ☐ = ☐

6. 5 + 2 = 7

☐ + ☐ = ☐

☐ − ☐ = ☐

☐ − ☐ = ☐

Counting to 20

Practice the Numbers

COUNT the cubes. Then TRACE each number and word.

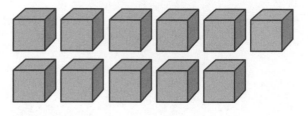

or

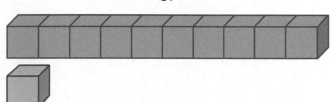

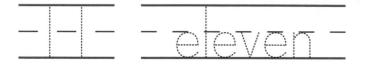

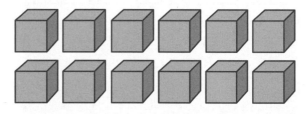

or

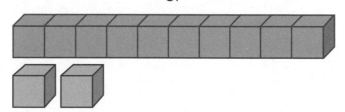

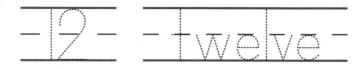

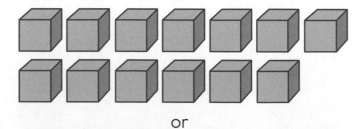

or

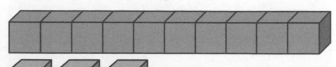

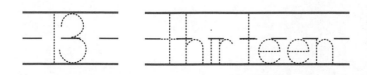

Chart Smart

This chart shows how many people like different foods for lunch. COUNT how many people like each kind of food. Then WRITE the number.

Pizza	
Sandwich	
Chili	
Hamburger	

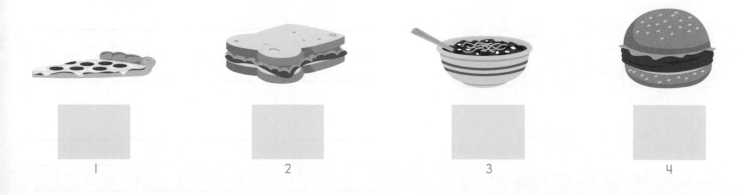

1   2   3   4

Counting to 20

Practice the Numbers

COUNT the cubes. Then TRACE each number and word.

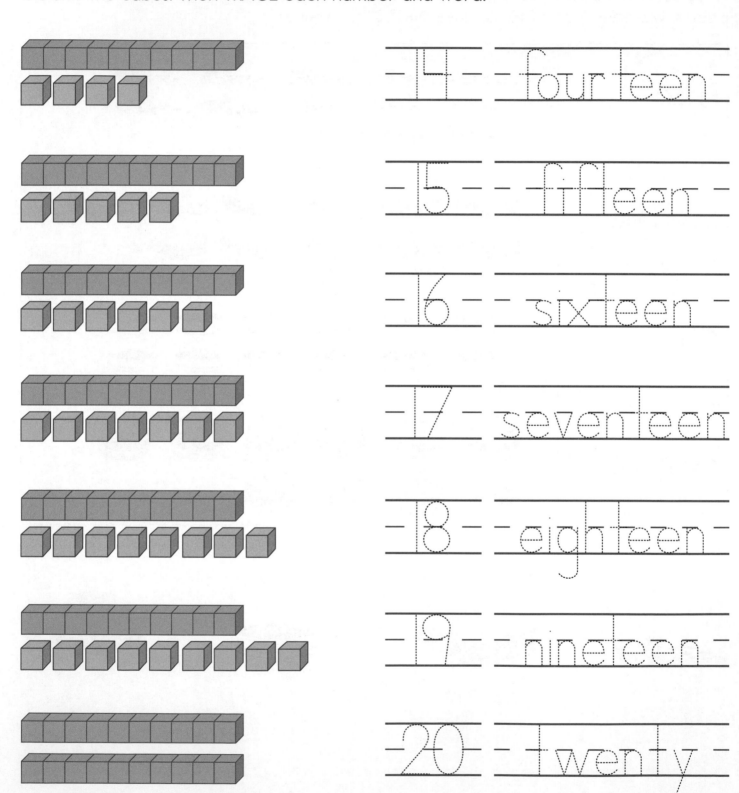

14 fourteen

15 fifteen

16 sixteen

17 seventeen

18 eighteen

19 nineteen

20 twenty

Loop It

LOOK at each number. CIRCLE the correct number of jellybeans to match the number.

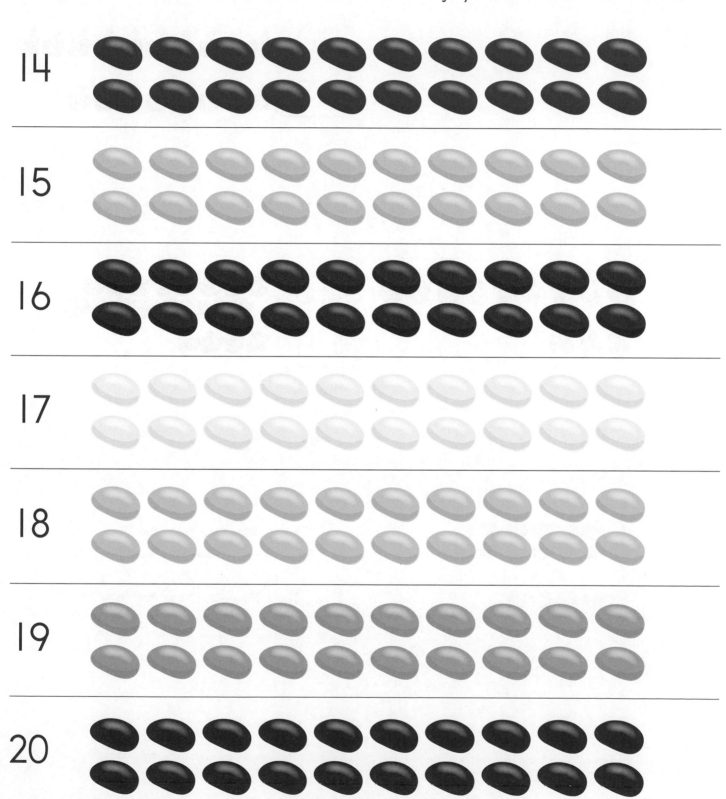

14

15

16

17

18

19

20

Picture It

WRITE each sum.

$$\begin{array}{r} 12 \\ + 2 \\ \hline \end{array}$$

1

$$\begin{array}{r} 10 \\ + 8 \\ \hline \end{array}$$

2

$$\begin{array}{r} 9 \\ + 3 \\ \hline \end{array}$$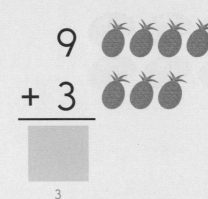

3

$$\begin{array}{r} 16 \\ + 4 \\ \hline \end{array}$$

4

$$\begin{array}{r} 14 \\ + 5 \\ \hline \end{array}$$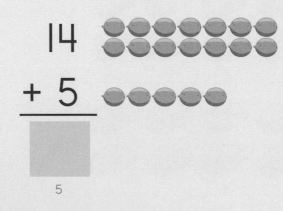

5

$$\begin{array}{r} 13 \\ + 6 \\ \hline \end{array}$$

6

Picture It

WRITE the number of gems. Then WRITE the sum.

1.

[ ] + [ ] = [ ]

2.

[ ] + [ ] = [ ]

3.

[ ] + [ ] = [ ]

4.

[ ] + [ ] = [ ]

5.

[ ] + [ ] = [ ]

6.

[ ] + [ ] = [ ]

Chart Smart

This chart shows how many kids like to play different sports. WRITE the number of kids who like each sport. Then ADD the numbers.

Basketball	🏀 🏀 🏀 🏀 🏀 🏀 🏀 🏀
Football	🏈 🏈 🏈 🏈 🏈 🏈 🏈
Hockey	🏒 🏒 🏒 🏒 🏒 🏒 🏒 🏒 🏒 🏒 🏒 🏒
Baseball	⚾ ⚾ ⚾ ⚾ ⚾ ⚾ ⚾ ⚾ ⚾
Soccer	⚽ ⚽ ⚽ ⚽ ⚽
Tennis	🎾 🎾 🎾 🎾 🎾 🎾 🎾 🎾

1. ☐ + ☐ = ☐

2. ☐ + ☐ = ☐

3. ☐ + ☐ = ☐

4. ☐ + ☐ = ☐

5. ☐ + ☐ = ☐

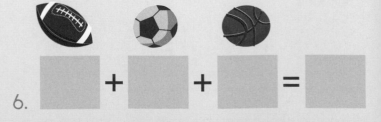

6. ☐ + ☐ + ☐ = ☐

Rock-Star Kids

ADD the scores of each performer.
CIRCLE the performer with the most points.

8	7	3

★★★★
★★★★   ★★★   ★★★

8	5	7

★★★★   ★★★★   ★★★★
★★★★   ★   ★★★

6	6	4

★★★★   ★★★★   ★★★★
★★   ★★

5	8	6

★★★★   ★★★★   ★★★★
★   ★★★★   ★★

Bug Collection

WRITE the missing number.

HINT: Count the bugs to help you.

1.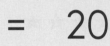

6 + ☐ = 18

2.

☐ + 3 = 20

3.

☐ + 5 = 11

4.

7 + ☐ = 13

5.

12 + ☐ = 14

6.

☐ + 9 = 17

It All Adds Up

WRITE each sum.

1.
$$10$$
$$+\ 3$$

2.
$$14$$
$$+\ 3$$

3.
$$9$$
$$+\ 5$$

4.
$$17$$
$$+\ 2$$

5.
$$13$$
$$+\ 6$$

6.
$$20$$
$$+\ 0$$

7.
$$8$$
$$+\ 9$$

8.
$$7$$
$$+\ 7$$

9.
$$11$$
$$+\ 9$$

10.
$$16$$
$$+\ 1$$

11.
$$7$$
$$+\ 5$$

12.
$$12$$
$$+\ 4$$

13.
$$15$$
$$+\ 3$$

14.
$$11$$
$$+\ 5$$

15.
$$13$$
$$+\ 0$$

16.
$$8$$
$$+\ 6$$

The Chocolate Eater

How many chocolates are left on the plate after the Chocolate Eater eats some?
WRITE the answer.

HINT: Cross off the number of eaten chocolates, and count how many are left.

1. 13 – 5 =

2. 17 – 4 =

3. 15 – 8 =

4. 20 – 9 =

Cracking Eggs

DRAW cracks on the eggs, and COUNT how many eggs are left. WRITE the number.

1.
$$\begin{array}{r} 12 \\ -\ 7 \\ \hline \end{array}$$

2.
$$\begin{array}{r} 18 \\ -\ 4 \\ \hline \end{array}$$

3.
$$\begin{array}{r} 14 \\ -\ 7 \\ \hline \end{array}$$

4.
$$\begin{array}{r} 11 \\ -\ 6 \\ \hline \end{array}$$

5.
$$\begin{array}{r} 16 \\ -\ 10 \\ \hline \end{array}$$

6.
$$\begin{array}{r} 19 \\ -\ 9 \\ \hline \end{array}$$

Chart Smart

This chart shows how many kids like different books. WRITE the number of kids who like different books. Then WRITE the difference.

Funniest Jokes	
Moving to Mars	
Diva Dreams	
Town and Farm	
Zombie Pirates	

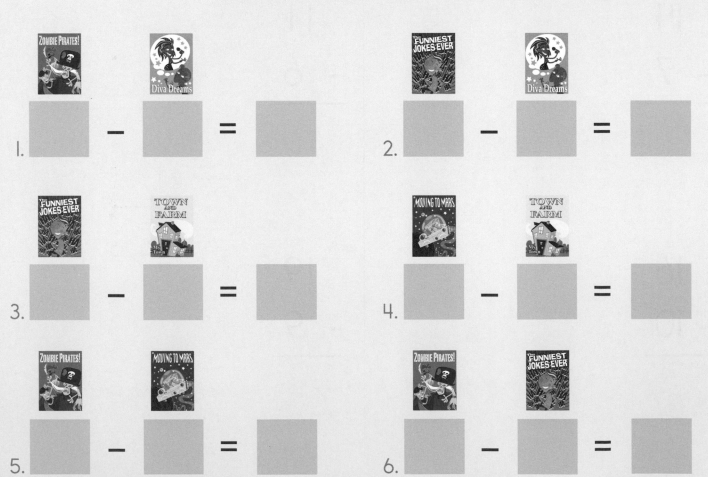

1. ☐ − ☐ = ☐

2. ☐ − ☐ = ☐

3. ☐ − ☐ = ☐

4. ☐ − ☐ = ☐

5. ☐ − ☐ = ☐

6. ☐ − ☐ = ☐

Balloon Pop

Each row shows how many balloons there were at the start of the party...and later after some popped. WRITE the number of balloons that popped.

1. 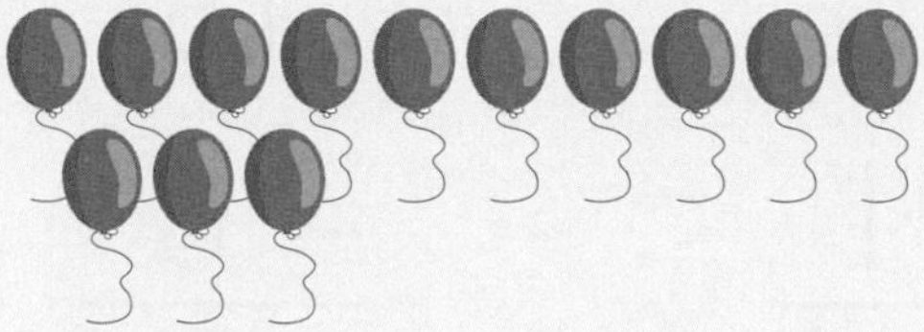 $-$ [ ] $=$

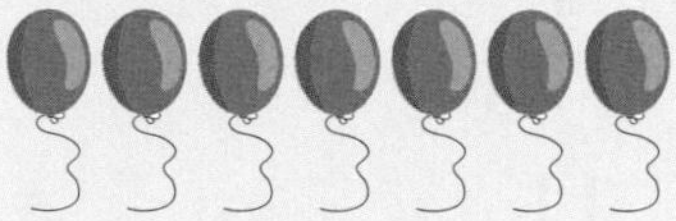

2. 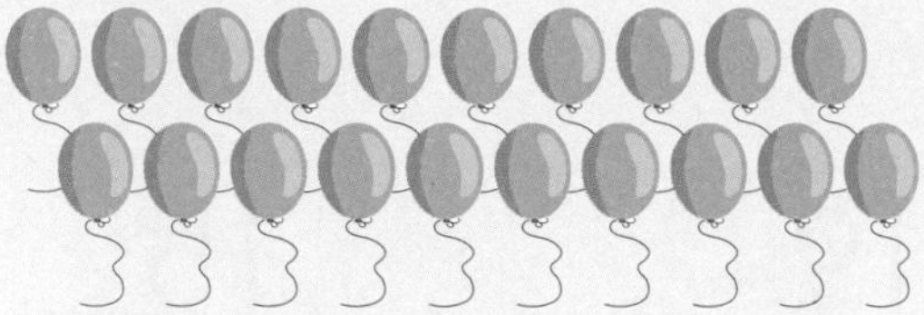 $-$ [ ] $=$

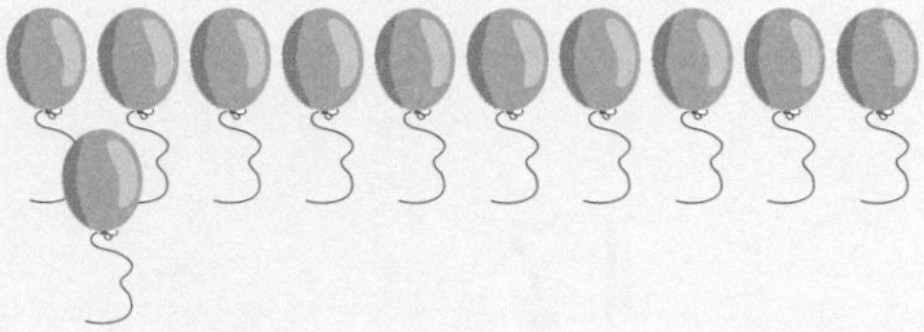

3. 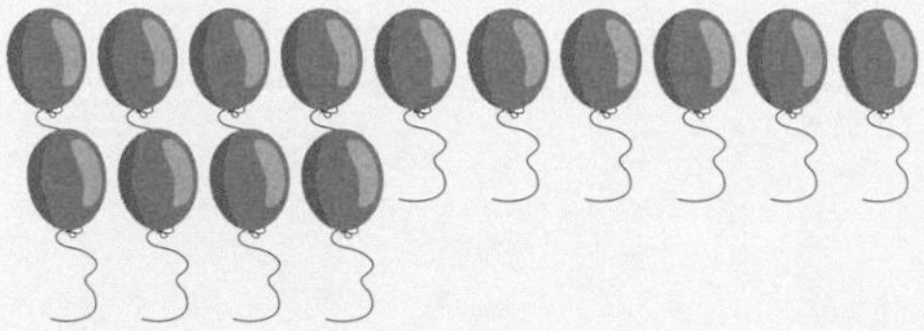 $-$ [ ] $=$

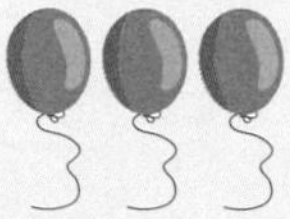

4. 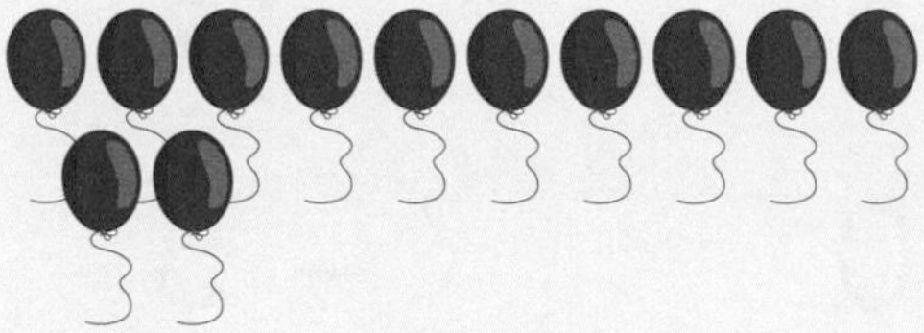 $-$ [ ] $=$

5. 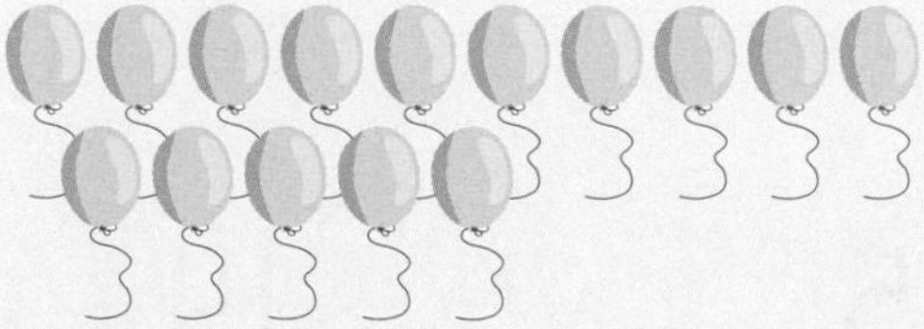 $-$ [ ] $=$

6. 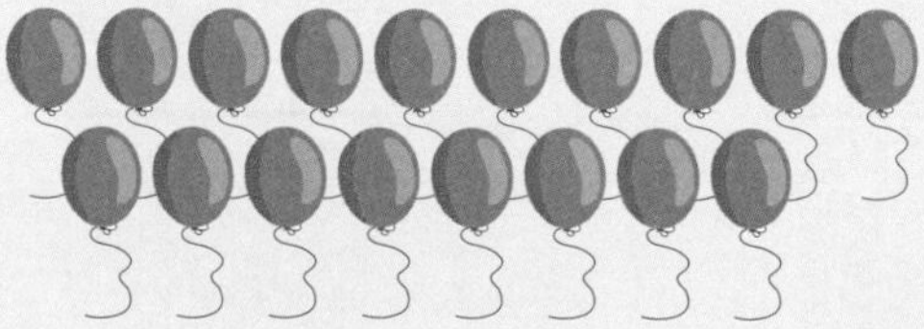 $-$ [ ] $=$

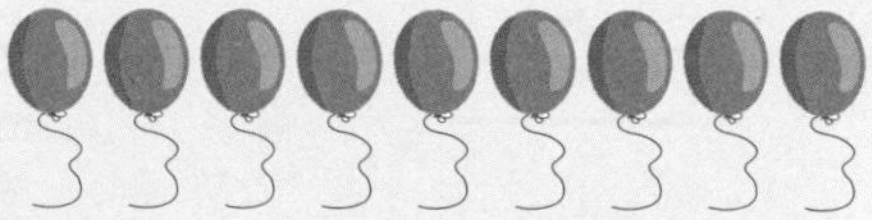

Subtracting Differences from 20

What's the Difference?

WRITE each difference.

1.
$$\begin{array}{r} 11 \\ -4 \\ \hline \end{array}$$

2.
$$\begin{array}{r} 16 \\ -7 \\ \hline \end{array}$$

3.
$$\begin{array}{r} 20 \\ -11 \\ \hline \end{array}$$

4.
$$\begin{array}{r} 18 \\ -8 \\ \hline \end{array}$$

5.
$$\begin{array}{r} 17 \\ -13 \\ \hline \end{array}$$

6.
$$\begin{array}{r} 14 \\ -0 \\ \hline \end{array}$$

7.
$$\begin{array}{r} 19 \\ -3 \\ \hline \end{array}$$

8.
$$\begin{array}{r} 15 \\ -14 \\ \hline \end{array}$$

9.
$$\begin{array}{r} 12 \\ -8 \\ \hline \end{array}$$

10.
$$\begin{array}{r} 20 \\ -6 \\ \hline \end{array}$$

11.
$$\begin{array}{r} 13 \\ -10 \\ \hline \end{array}$$

12.
$$\begin{array}{r} 17 \\ -5 \\ \hline \end{array}$$

13.
$$\begin{array}{r} 18 \\ -16 \\ \hline \end{array}$$

14.
$$\begin{array}{r} 11 \\ -1 \\ \hline \end{array}$$

15.
$$\begin{array}{r} 15 \\ -5 \\ \hline \end{array}$$

16.
$$\begin{array}{r} 14 \\ -8 \\ \hline \end{array}$$

Fact Finder

COMPLETE each fact family.

1. 9 + 10 = 19

    ▢ + ▢ = ▢
    ▢ − ▢ = ▢
    ▢ − ▢ = ▢

2. 8 + 3 = 11

    ▢ + ▢ = ▢
    ▢ − ▢ = ▢
    ▢ − ▢ = ▢

3. 5 + 9 = 14

    ▢ + ▢ = ▢
    ▢ − ▢ = ▢
    ▢ − ▢ = ▢

4. 11 + 6 = 17

    ▢ + ▢ = ▢
    ▢ − ▢ = ▢
    ▢ − ▢ = ▢

5. 10 + 8 = 18

    ▢ + ▢ = ▢
    ▢ − ▢ = ▢
    ▢ − ▢ = ▢

6. 14 + 2 = 16

    ▢ + ▢ = ▢
    ▢ − ▢ = ▢
    ▢ − ▢ = ▢

Beetlemania

COUNT the beetles. Then WRITE the number of beetles.

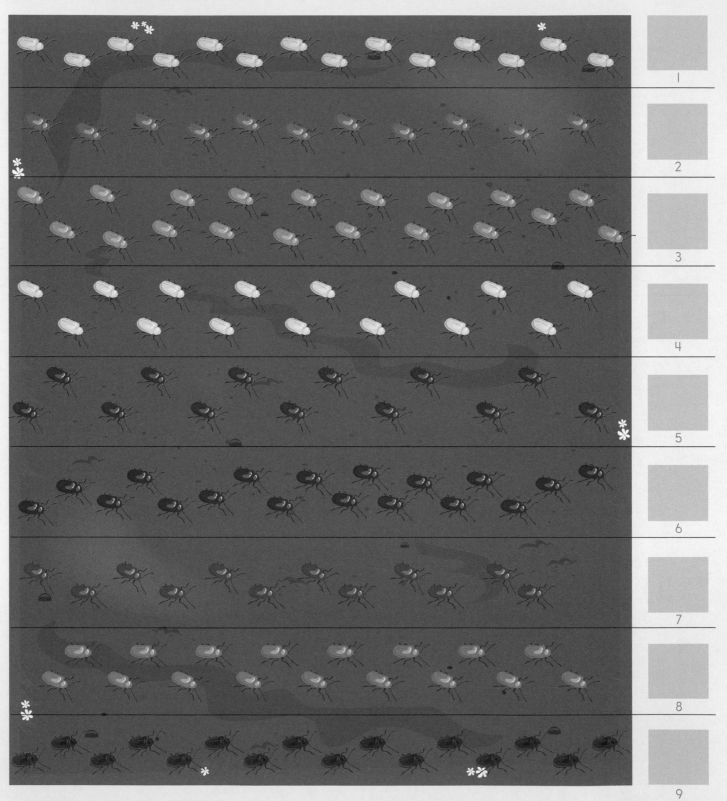

1

2

3

4

5

6

7

8

9

Unit Rewind

WRITE each sum or difference.

1. 15
    + 4
    ▢

2. 8
    + 7
    ▢

3. 12
    + 8
    ▢

4. 10
    + 5
    ▢

5. 18
    + 1
    ▢

6. 11
    + 6
    ▢

7. 9
    + 3
    ▢

8. 19
    + 0
    ▢

9. 13
    − 7
    ▢

10. 18
    −14
    ▢

11. 17
    − 8
    ▢

12. 20
    − 3
    ▢

13. 16
    − 4
    ▢

14. 15
    −11
    ▢

15. 19
    −10
    ▢

16. 16
    − 0
    ▢

Unit Rewind

WRITE the missing number in each problem.

1. $5 + \boxed{} = 13$

2. $\boxed{} + 12 = 20$

3. $\boxed{} + 1 = 11$

4. $9 + \boxed{} = 18$

5. $10 + \boxed{} = 16$

6. $\boxed{} + 6 = 17$

7. $\boxed{} - 1 = 12$

8. $\boxed{} - 5 = 15$

9. $19 - \boxed{} = 2$

10. $\boxed{} - 2 = 16$

11. $\boxed{} - 6 = 6$

12. $14 - \boxed{} = 1$

Fact Finder

COMPLETE each fact family.

1. 10 + 3 = 13

☐ + ☐ = ☐
☐ − ☐ = ☐
☐ − ☐ = ☐

2. 13 + 7 = 20

☐ + ☐ = ☐
☐ − ☐ = ☐
☐ − ☐ = ☐

3. 8 + 4 = 12

☐ + ☐ = ☐
☐ − ☐ = ☐
☐ − ☐ = ☐

4. 13 + 6 = 19

☐ + ☐ = ☐
☐ − ☐ = ☐
☐ − ☐ = ☐

5. 11 + 5 = 16

☐ + ☐ = ☐
☐ − ☐ = ☐
☐ − ☐ = ☐

6. 14 + 3 = 17

☐ + ☐ = ☐
☐ − ☐ = ☐
☐ − ☐ = ☐

Counting to 100

Practice the Numbers

TRACE each number and word.

30 thirty

40 forty

50 fifty

60 sixty

70 seventy

80 eighty

90 ninety

100 one hundred

7

Match Up

DRAW lines to connect the numbers and pictures that go together.

80

30

50

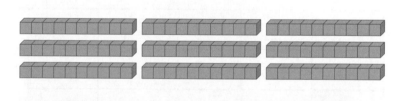

90

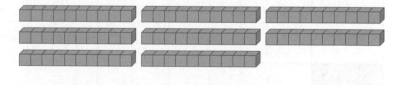

60

100

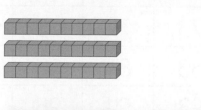

40

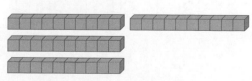

70

Color Clash

COLOR the numbers in the chart using the colors shown.

41	
28	
67	
95	
50	

33	
79	
84	
16	
72	

1	2	3	4	5	6	7	8	9	10
11	12	13	14	15	16	17	18	19	20
21	22	23	24	25	26	27	28	29	30
31	32	33	34	35	36	37	38	39	40
41	42	43	44	45	46	47	48	49	50
51	52	53	54	55	56	57	58	59	60
61	62	63	64	65	66	67	68	69	70
71	72	73	74	75	76	77	78	79	80
81	82	83	84	85	86	87	88	89	90
91	92	93	94	95	96	97	98	99	100

Holey Hundreds!

WRITE the missing numbers on the chart.

1	2	3	4	5	6	7		9	10
11		13	14	15	16		18	19	20
21	22	23		25	26	27	28	29	
31	32	33	34	35	36	37		39	40
41	42		44	45	46	47	48	49	50
	52	53	54	55		57	58	59	
61	62	63	64		66	67	68	69	70
71		73	74	75	76	77	78		80
81	82	83		85	86	87	88	89	90
	92	93	94	95	96	97		99	100

Bug Collection

CIRCLE groups of ten to help you count. Then WRITE the number of bugs.

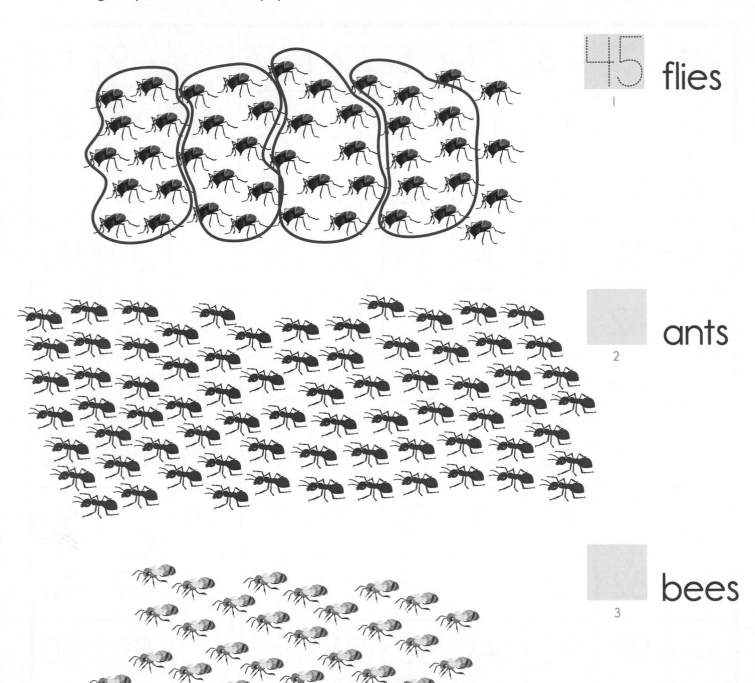

45 flies

1

ants

2

bees

3

 ladybugs

 butterflies

 roaches

Get in Place

WRITE how many tens and ones you see. Then WRITE the number they make.

1.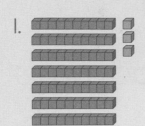

Tens	Ones
7	3

73

2.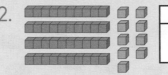

Tens	Ones

3.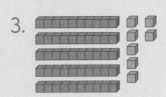

Tens	Ones

4.

Tens	Ones

5.

Tens	Ones

6.

Tens	Ones

7.

Tens	Ones

8.

Tens	Ones

9.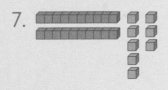

Tens	Ones

10.

Tens	Ones

Match Up

DRAW lines to connect the numbers and pictures that go together.

87

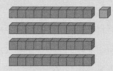

29

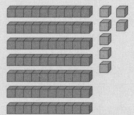

41

77

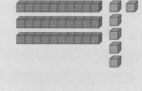

65

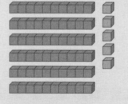

36

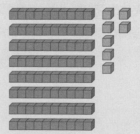

Ones, Tens & Hundreds

Loop It

CIRCLE the correct number of tens and ones to match the number.

34

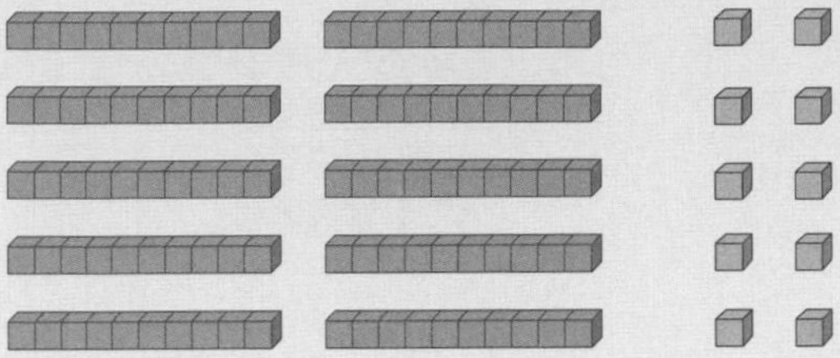

81

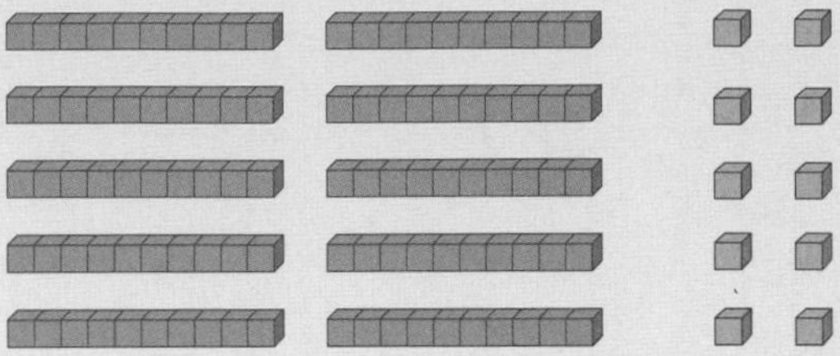

98

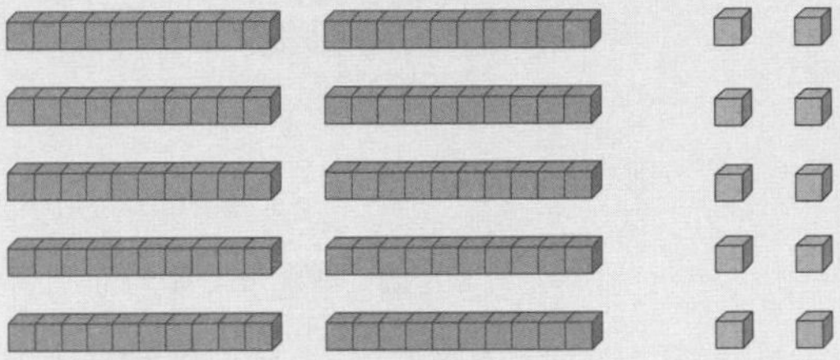

44

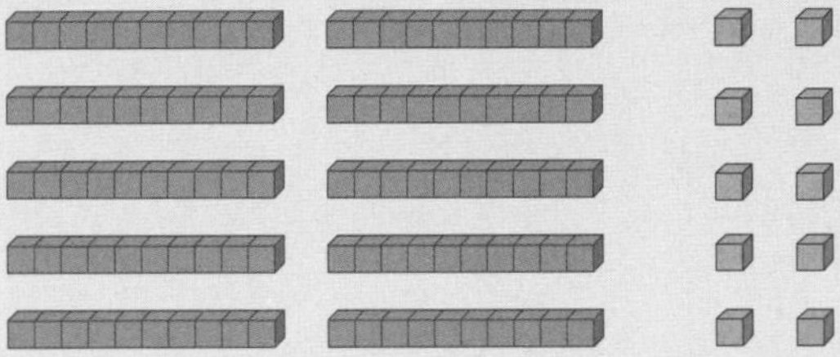

27

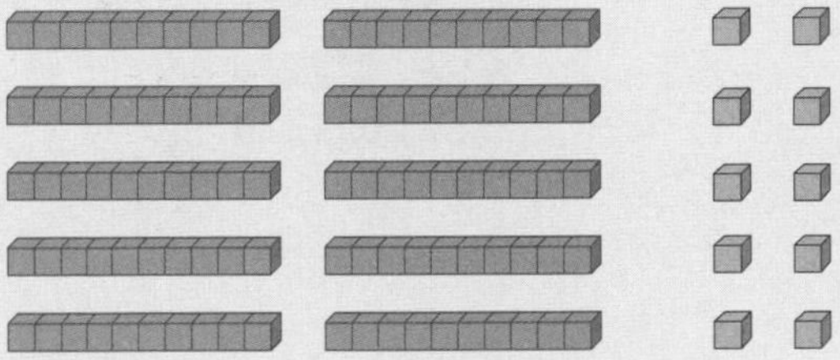

75

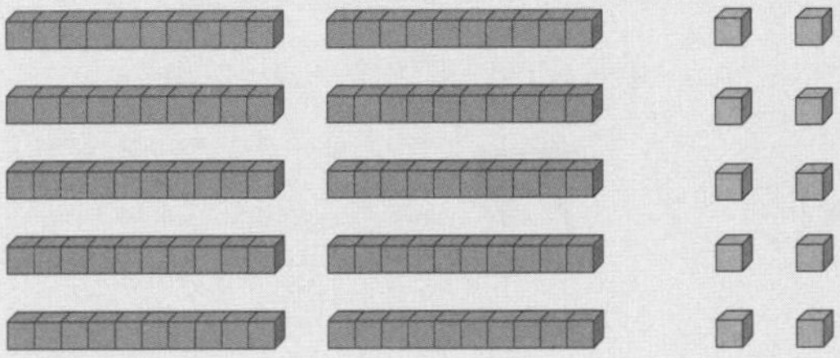

59

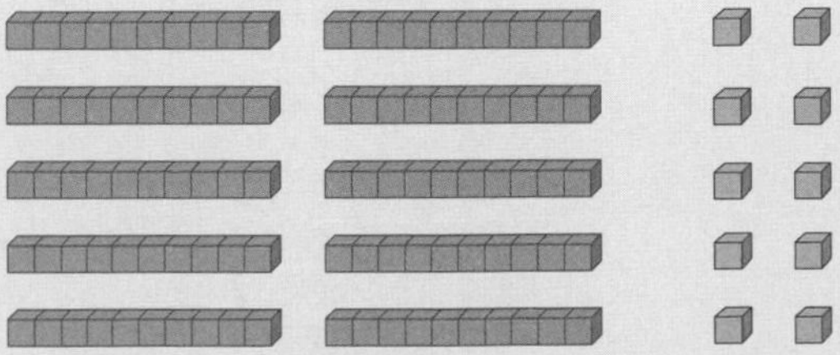

62

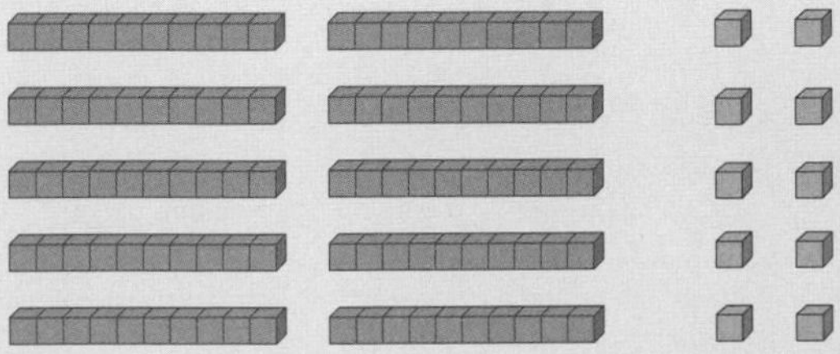

Get in Place

WRITE how many hundreds, tens, and ones you see. Then WRITE the number they make.

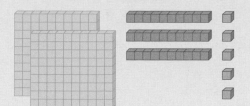

Hundreds	Tens	Ones

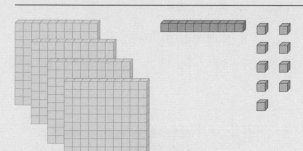

Hundreds	Tens	Ones

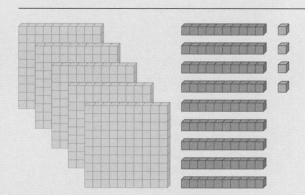

Hundreds	Tens	Ones

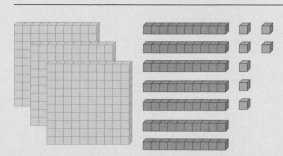

Hundreds	Tens	Ones

Number Match

CIRCLE the picture in each row that matches the number.

628

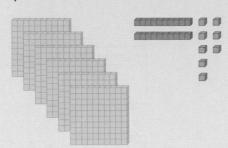 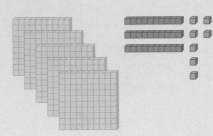

173

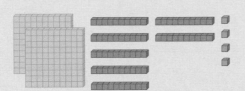 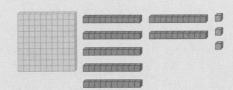

466

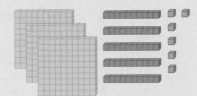 

381

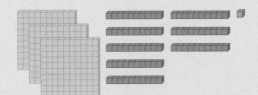 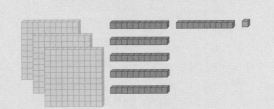

535

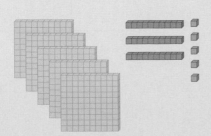 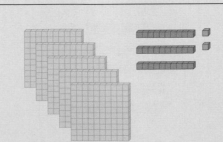

Ones, Tens & Hundreds

Write It

WRITE the number for each picture.

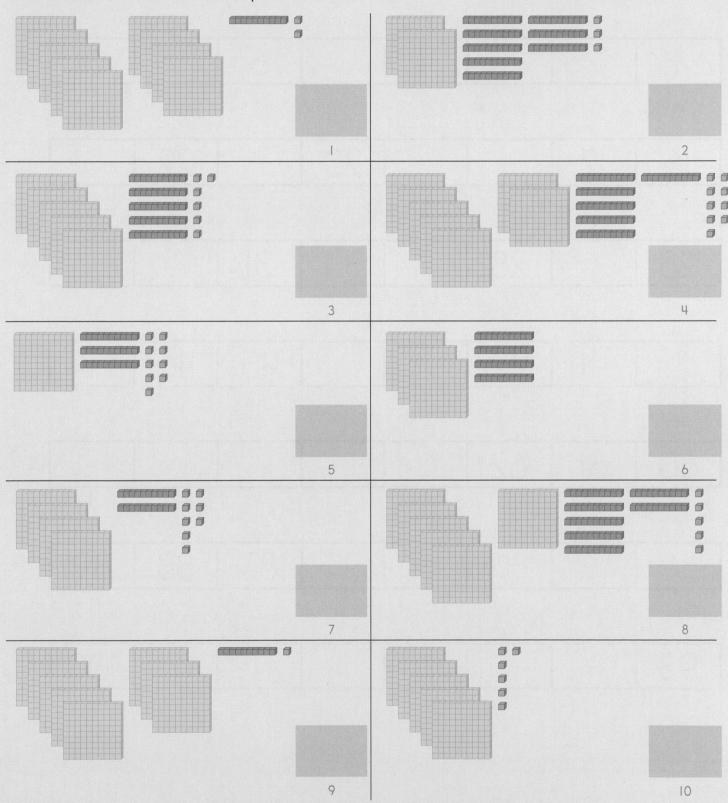

1

2

3

4

5

6

7

8

9

10

Number Lines & Patterns

Pattern Patch

WRITE the missing numbers to finish each pattern.

| 1 | 2 | | 4 | | 6 | | 8 |

| 16 | 17 | | | 20 | | 22 | |

| 26 | | 28 | | 30 | 31 | | |

| | 41 | 42 | | | 45 | 46 | |

| 60 | 61 | 62 | | | | | |

| | | | | | 87 | 88 | 89 |

| 93 | | | | | | | 100 |

Get in Line

WRITE the missing numbers on each number line.

0   1   2   3   4   5   6   7

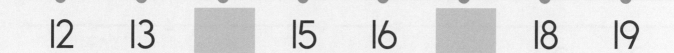

12   13   ☐   15   16   ☐   18   19

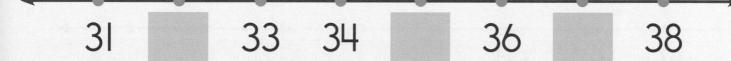

31   ☐   33   34   ☐   36   ☐   38

53   54   55   ☐   57   ☐   59   60

☐   66   67   ☐   69   70   ☐   72

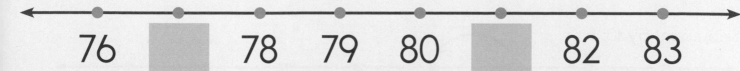

76   ☐   78   79   80   ☐   82   83

Number Lines & Patterns

Get in Line

WRITE the missing numbers on each number line, skip counting by 2, 5, and 10.

Skip count by 2:

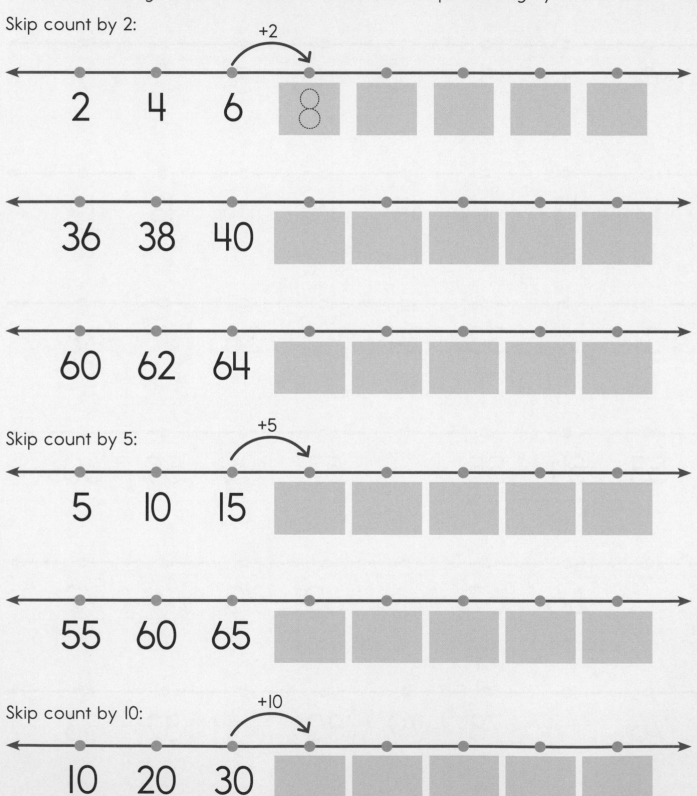

Skip count by 5:

Skip count by 10:

Color Clash

Starting at number 2, skip count by 2 and COLOR the squares red.
Starting at number 5, skip count by 10 and COLOR the squares blue.

1	2	3	4	5	6	7	8	9	10
11	12	13	14	15	16	17	18	19	20
21	22	23	24	25	26	27	28	29	30
31	32	33	34	35	36	37	38	39	40
41	42	43	44	45	46	47	48	49	50
51	52	53	54	55	56	57	58	59	60
61	62	63	64	65	66	67	68	69	70
71	72	73	74	75	76	77	78	79	80
81	82	83	84	85	86	87	88	89	90
91	92	93	94	95	96	97	98	99	100

Which One?

CIRCLE the picture that has **more** than the other.

Which One?

CIRCLE the picture that has **less** than the other.

Comparing Numbers

Circle It

CIRCLE the number that is **more** than the number shown in the picture.

1.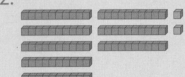

62   79

2.

87   80

3.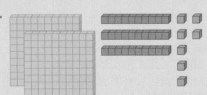

106   117

4.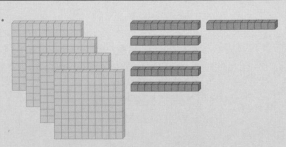

228   240

5.

462   440

Circle It

CIRCLE the number that is **less** than the number shown in the picture.

1.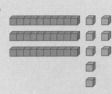

32   39

2.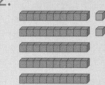

48   55

3.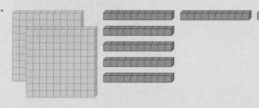

270   259

4.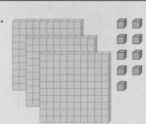

298   310

5.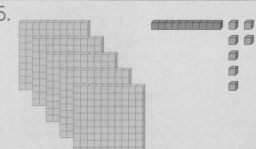

519   515

Load the Truck

DRAW a line to connect each truck with the right box.

HINT: Group objects to help you count what is on each truck.

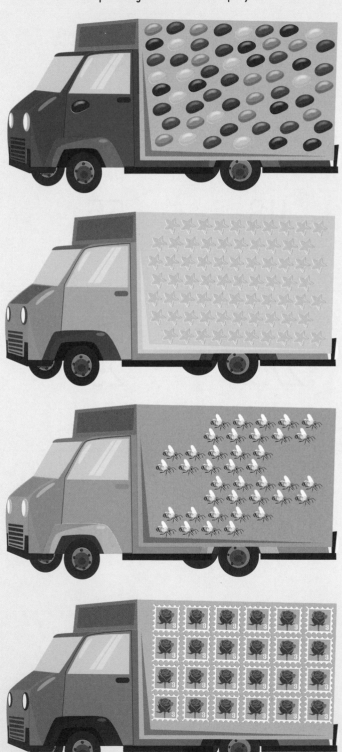

Picture It

WRITE the number for each picture.

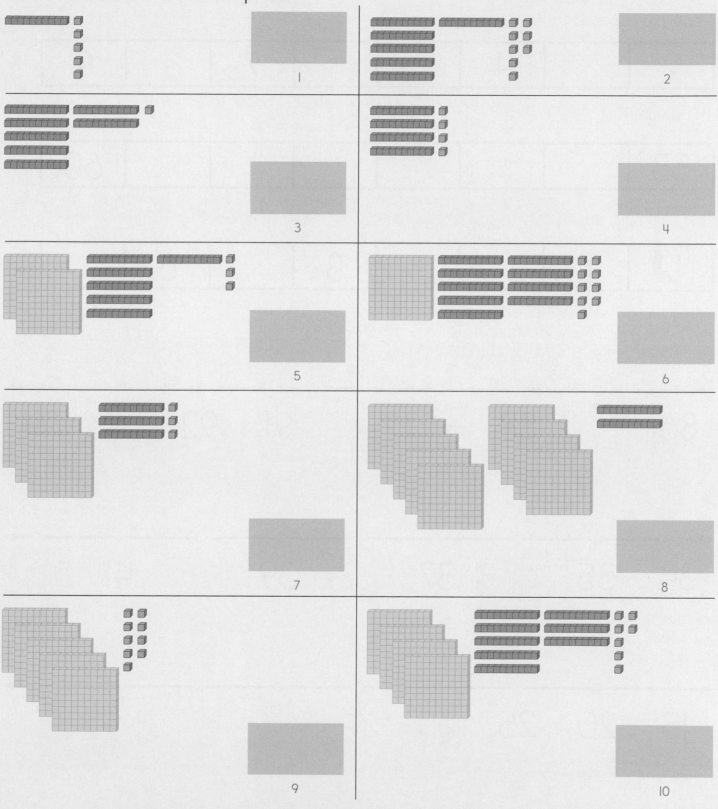

1

2

3

4

5

6

7

8

9

10

Review

Get in Line

WRITE the missing numbers.

| 2 | | 4 | | | 7 | | 9 |

| 53 | | | | | | | 60 |

| 12 | 11 | | | 8 | | 6 | |

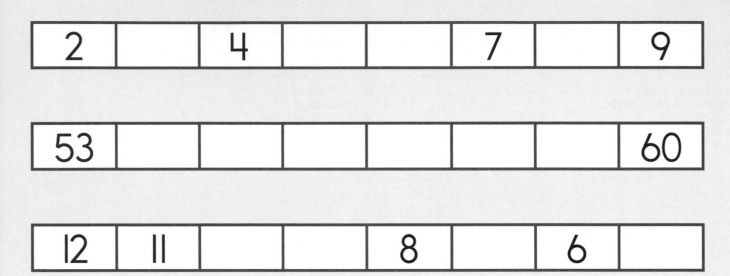

86 ___ 88 ___ ___ 91 92 ___ 94

34 35 ___ 37 ___ 39 ___ 41 ___

15 20 25 ___ ___ ___ ___ ___ ___

Circle It

CIRCLE the picture that has **more** than the other.

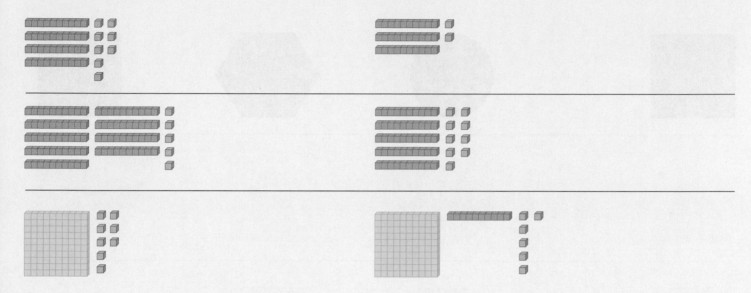

CIRCLE the number that is **less** than the number shown in the picture.

	49	55
	86	76
	327	340
	631	628

Drawing & Comparing Shapes

Find the Same

CIRCLE the shape in each row that is the same shape as the first shape.

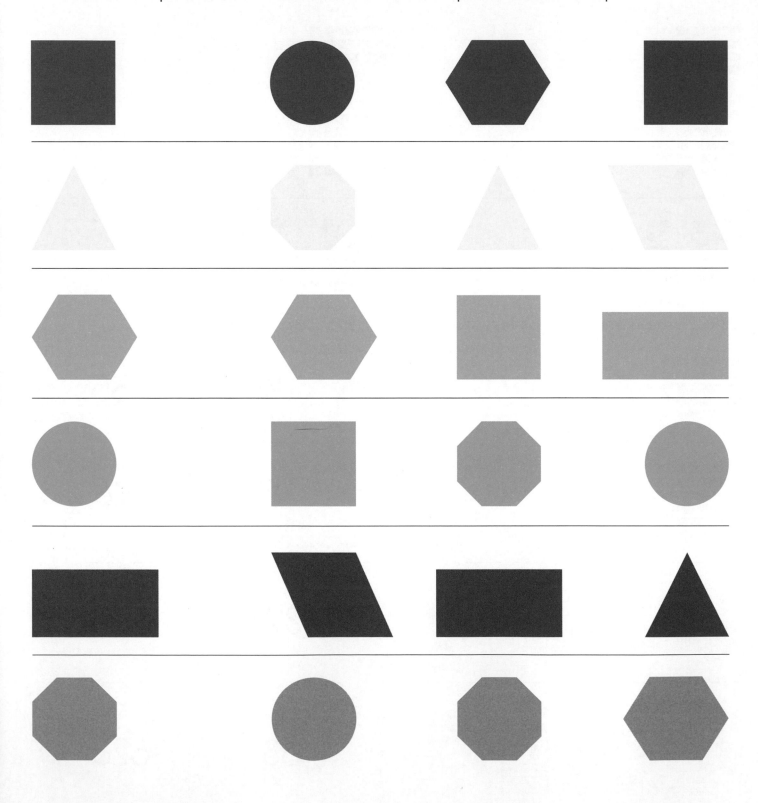

Match Up

DRAW lines to connect the shapes that are the same.

Drawing & Comparing Shapes

Shape Up

DRAW a shape that is the same as the one shown.

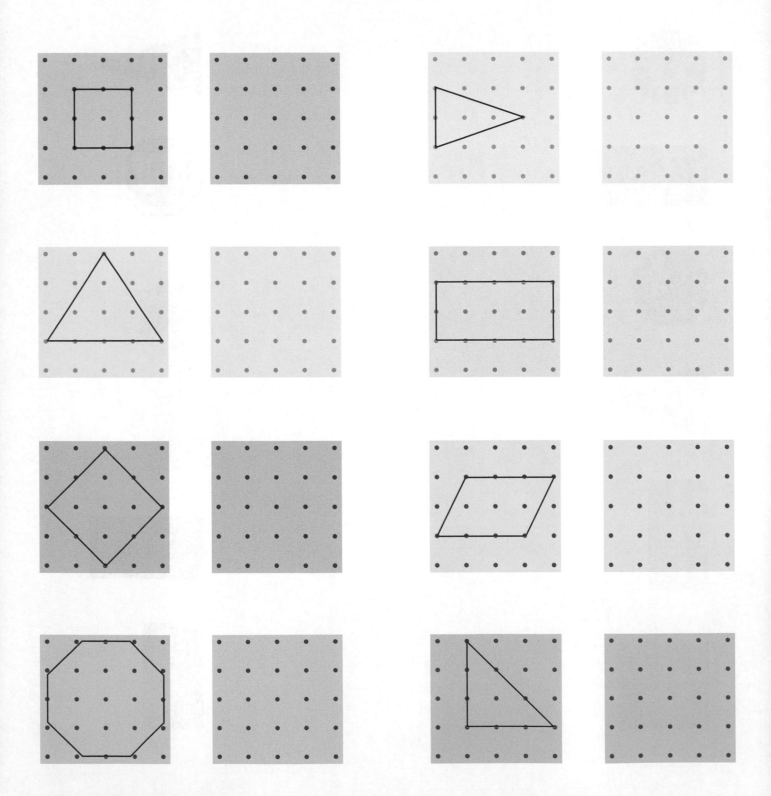

Odd One Out

CROSS OUT the picture in each row that does **not** go with the others.

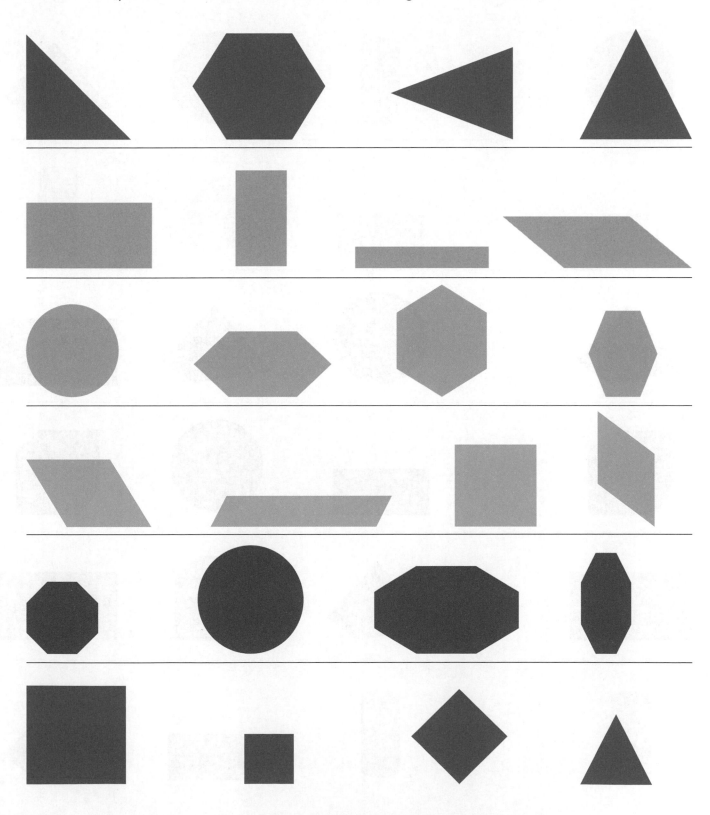

Drawing & Comparing Shapes

Find the Same

CIRCLE the shape in each row that is the same shape as the first shape.

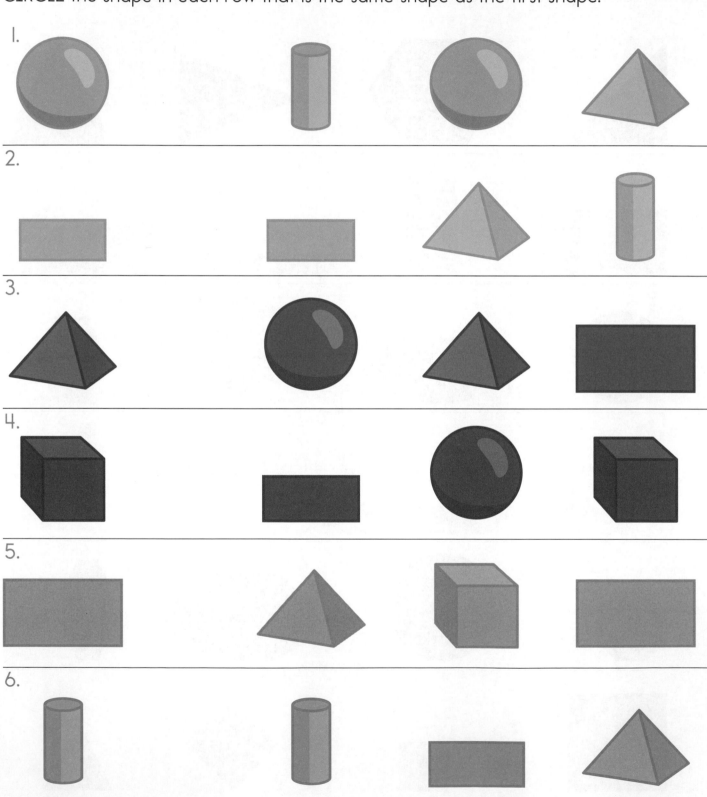

Hide and Seek

LOOK at the shapes. DRAW a line to connect each shape with the object in the picture that has the same shape.

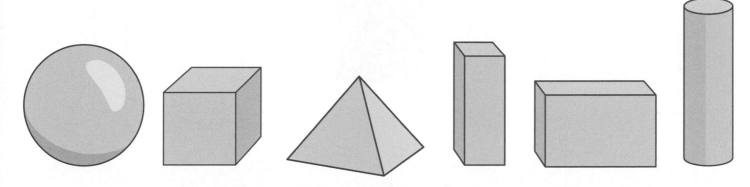

Shape Shifters

COLOR all of the shapes that are the same shape as the top shape.

Match Up

DRAW lines to connect the layered shapes with the separated shapes.

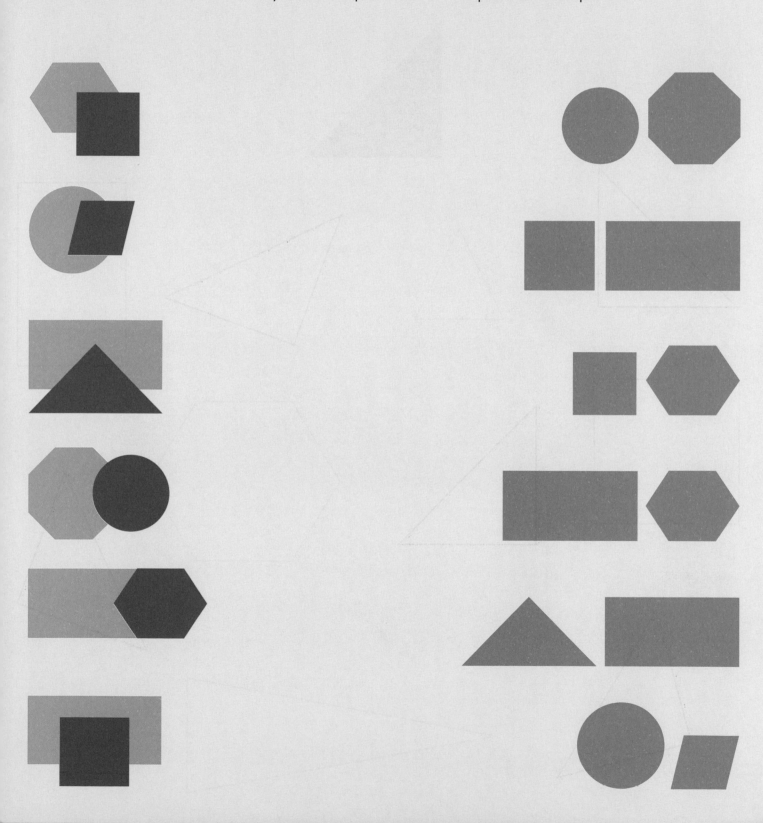

Shape Shifters

COLOR all of the shapes that are the same size and shape as the top shape.

Match Up

DRAW a line to connect each shape that has been cut in half with its matching whole shape.

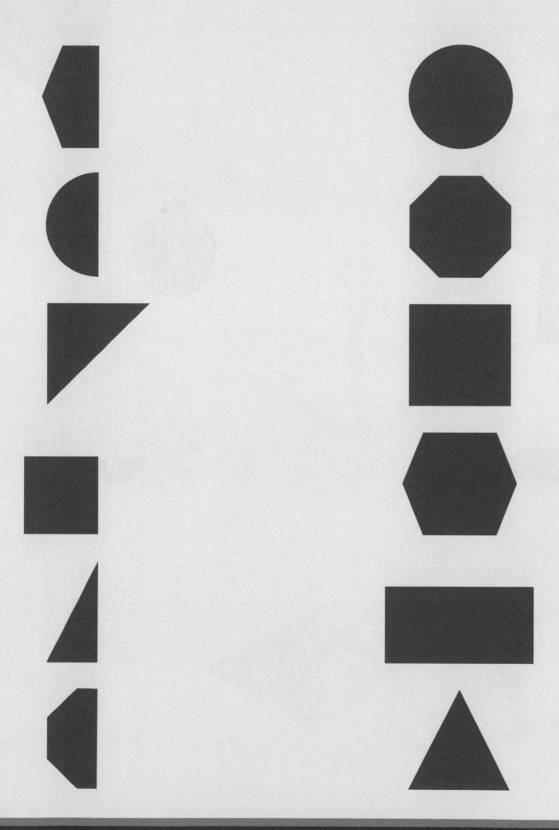

Symmetry

Mirror, Mirror

A shape has **symmetry** if a line can divide the shape so each half is a mirror image of the other. DRAW a line of symmetry through each picture.

Line of symmetry

Example:

Mirror, Mirror

CIRCLE the letter in each pair that has symmetry.

A P   J O

L Y   X F

Z U   S W

K Q   R D

Symmetry

Color Flip

COLOR the pictures so they are symmetrical.

Shape Up

DRAW the mirror image of each shape, making it symmetrical.

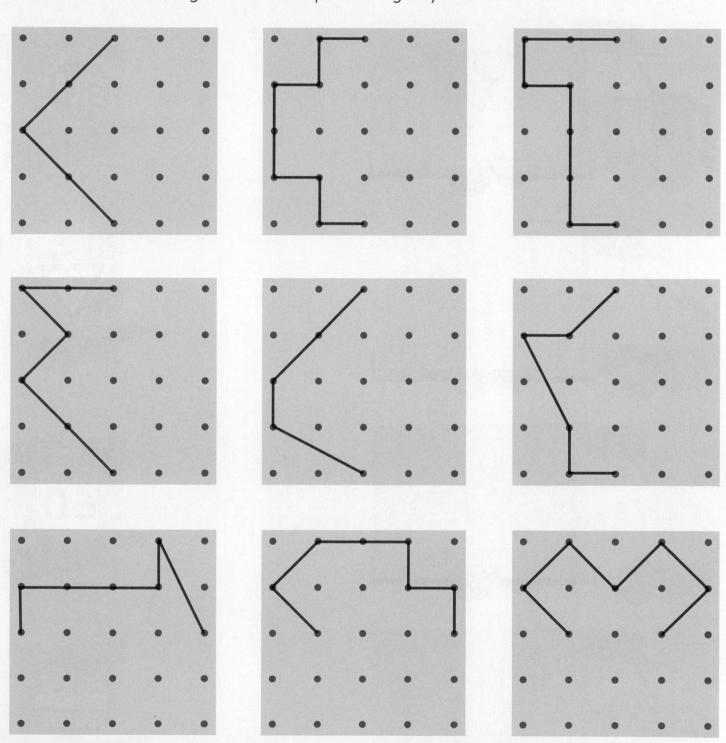

Load the Truck

DRAW a line to connect each truck with the right loading dock.

Load the Truck

DRAW a line to connect each truck with the right loading dock.

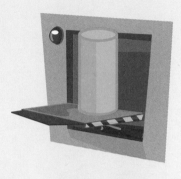

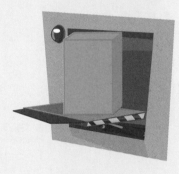

Shape Up

CROSS OUT the picture in each row that does **not** go with the others.

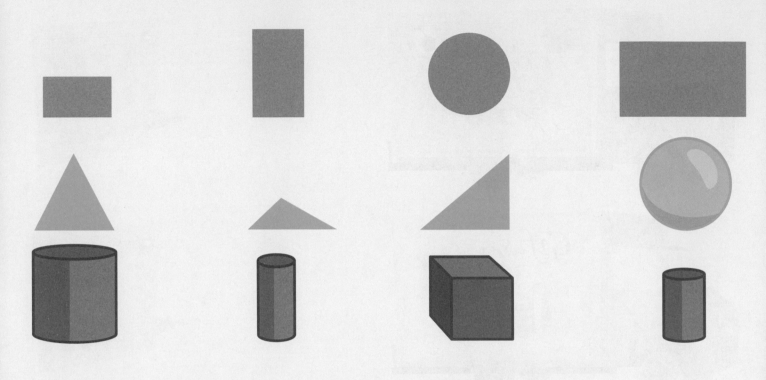

COLOR the shape that is the same size and shape as the first shape.

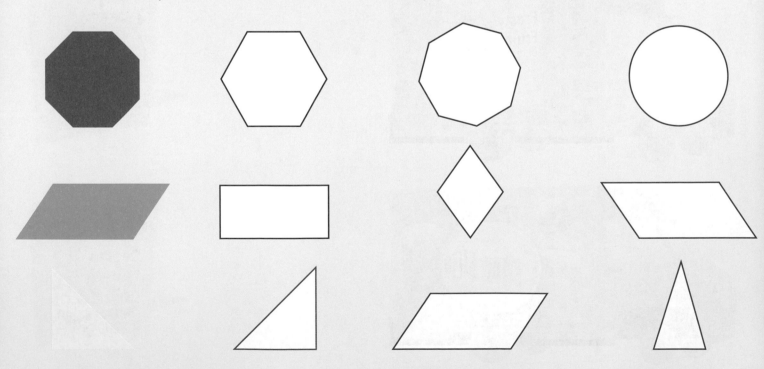

Mirror, Mirror

CIRCLE the shapes that have symmetry.

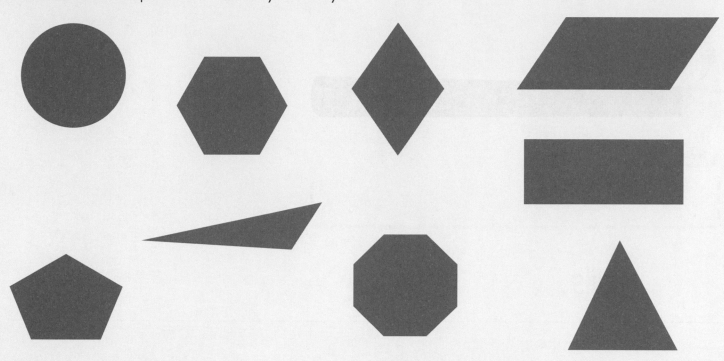

DRAW the mirror image of each shape, making it symmetrical.

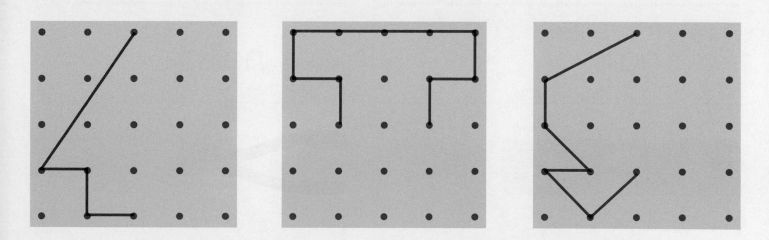

Measure Up

MEASURE the length of each object by the number of nails you can line up end to end.

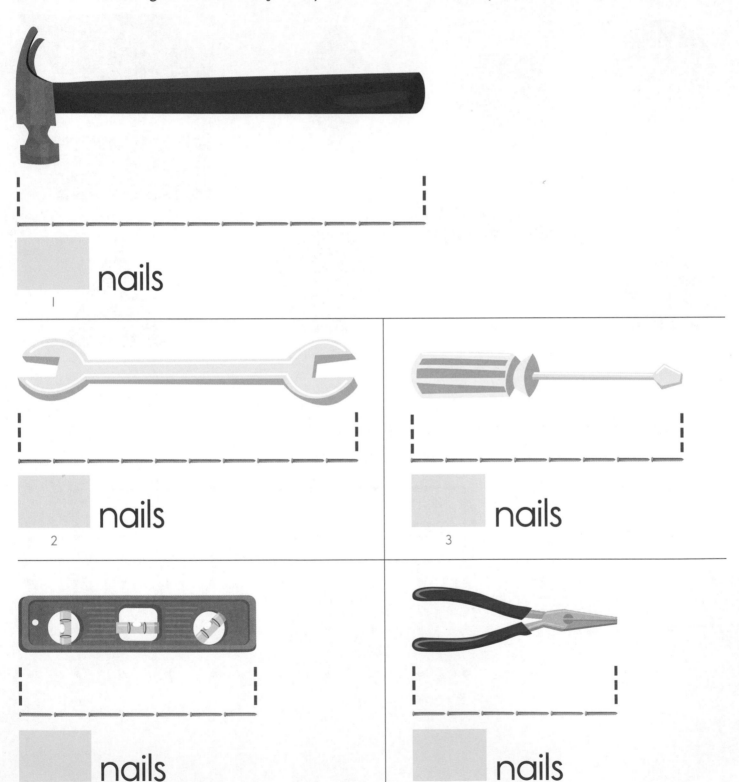

nails

1

nails

2

nails

3

nails

4

nails

5

Measure Up

MEASURE the length of each object in paper clips.

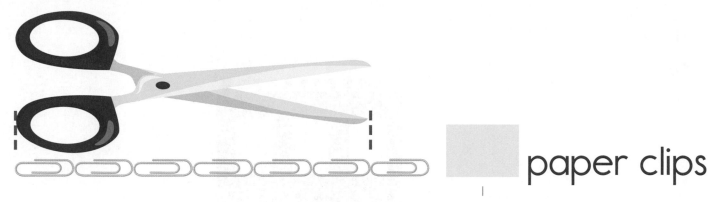

paper clips

1

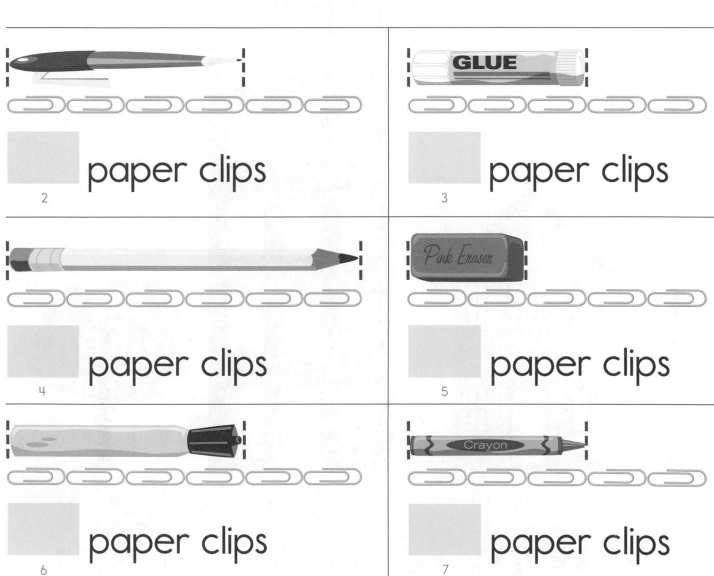

paper clips

2

paper clips

3

paper clips

4

paper clips

5

paper clips

6

paper clips

7

Measure Up

MEASURE the height of each object in people.

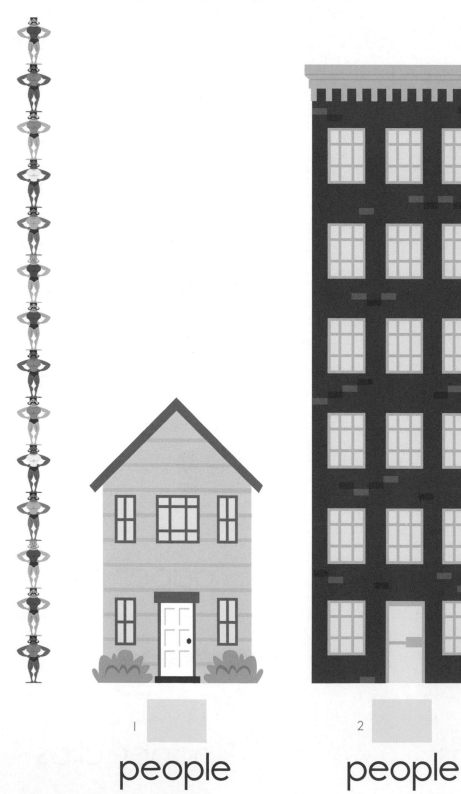

1 [ ] people

2 [ ] people

3 [ ] people

Penny Line Up

LINE UP pennies and MEASURE each object.

pennies

1

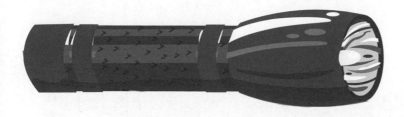

pennies

2

pennies

3

Inches & Centimeters

Measure Up

MEASURE the length of each object in inches.

 inches

 inches

 inches

 inches

Measure Up

MEASURE the length of each object in centimeters.

	1
	centimeters

	2
	centimeters

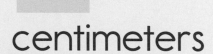

	3
	centimeters

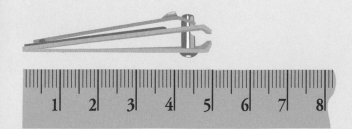

	4
	centimeters

Inches & Centimeters

Rulers Rule

MEASURE each worm with a ruler. COLOR the worms according to the chart.

1 inch		4 inches	
2 inches		5 inches	
3 inches		6 inches	

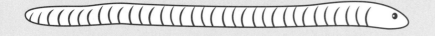

Rulers Rule

MEASURE with a ruler. DRAW a line to cut each piece of yarn to the correct length.

5 centimeters

|←— 5 centimeters —→|

14 centimeters

9 centimeters

11 centimeters

4 centimeters

7 centimeters

Approximation & Estimation

Measure Up

WRITE the approximate length of each fish in inches and centimeters.

HINT: To find the approximate length, measure each fish and find the closest number on the ruler.

1.

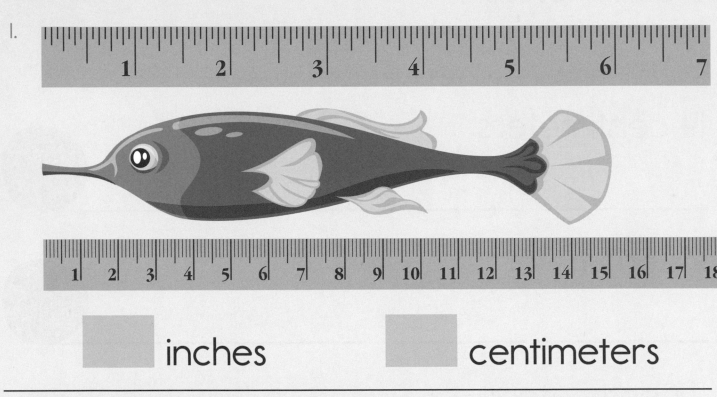

inches   centimeters

2.

inches   centimeters

Rulers Rule

MEASURE the height of each plant and its pot with a ruler. WRITE the approximate height of each plant in inches and centimeters.

1.

☐ inches
☐ centimeters

2.

☐ inches
☐ centimeters

3.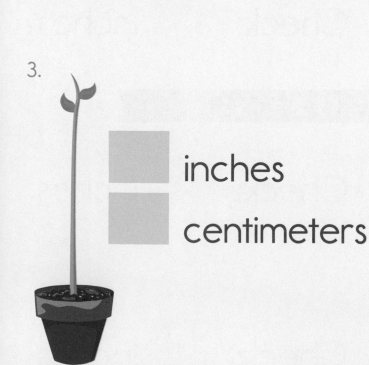

☐ inches
☐ centimeters

4.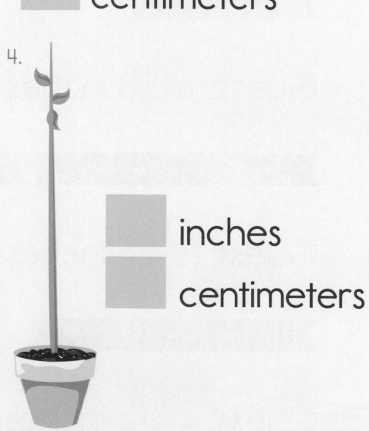

☐ inches
☐ centimeters

Approximation & Estimation

Rulers Rule

The red ribbon is 4 inches long. GUESS the length of each ribbon in inches. Then MEASURE each ribbon with a ruler to check your guess.

1. Guess: ___ inches   Check: ___ inches

2. Guess: ___ inches   Check: ___ inches

3. Guess: ___ inches   Check: ___ inches

4. Guess: ___ inches   Check: ___ inches

Rulers Rule

The snake at the top is 12 centimeters long. GUESS the length of each snake in centimeters (cm). Then MEASURE each snake with a ruler to check your guess.

1.

Guess: ☐ cm   Check: ☐ cm

2.

Guess: ☐ cm   Check: ☐ cm

3.

Guess: ☐ cm   Check: ☐ cm

4.

Guess: ☐ cm   Check: ☐ cm

Beetlemania

About how many beetles long is each object? WRITE your answer.

1.

about beetles

2.

about beetles

3.

about beetles

4.

about beetles

5.

about beetles

Rulers Rule

MEASURE each object in inches (in.) or centimeters (cm).

about [ ] in.

1

about [ ] in.

2

about [ ] cm

3

about [ ] cm

4

97

Telling Time in Hours

What Time Is It?

WRITE the time on each clock in two different ways.

Example:

5:00

five o'clock

1. :00

o'clock

2. :00

o'clock

3. :00

o'clock

4. :00

o'clock

5. :00

o'clock

6. :00

o'clock

Watch It!

DRAW a line to connect each watch to a clock that shows the same time.

Telling Time in Hours

Give Me a Hand

DRAW the hour hand to match the time.

1. ## 11:00

2. ## 6:00

3. ## 3:00

4. ## 10:00

5. ## 7:00

6. ## 9:00

7. ## 4:00

8. ## 1:00

Passing the Time

DRAW the time on the last clock to complete the pattern.

1.

2.

3.

4.

Telling Time in Half Hours

What Time Is It?

WRITE the time on each clock.

Example:

2:30

1.

⬜ : ⬜

2.

⬜ : ⬜

3.

⬜ : ⬜

4.

⬜ : ⬜

5.

⬜ : ⬜

6.

⬜ : ⬜

Watch It!

DRAW a line to connect each watch to a clock that shows the same time.

Telling Time in Half Hours

Give Me a Hand

DRAW the hour and minute hands to match the time.

5:30

12:30

8:30

1:30

2:30

4:30

11:30

3:30

Passing the Time

DRAW the time on the last clock to complete the pattern.

1.

2.

3.

4.

It's about Time

WRITE the time on each clock.

1.

☐ : ☐

2.

☐ : ☐

3.

☐ : ☐

4.

☐ : ☐

5.

☐ : ☐

6.

☐ : ☐

7.

☐ : ☐

8.

☐ : ☐

Passing the Time

DRAW the hour and minute hands to match the time.

1.
11:30

2.
7:00

3.
2:00

4.
8:30

DRAW the time on the last clock to complete the pattern.

5.

10:30

12:30

2:30

6.

Coin Values

Which One?

CIRCLE the group of coins that matches each number.

 1¢
penny

 **5¢**
nickel

 10¢
dime

 **25¢**
quarter

5¢	13¢

7¢	**14¢**

23¢	**31¢**

Match Up

DRAW lines to connect coins with the same value.

Coin Values

Money Bags

WRITE the value of the coin combination on the bag.

1.

2.

3.

4.

5.

6.

Odd One Out

CROSS OUT the picture or number in each row that does not match the others.

Using Coins

Pay Up

CIRCLE the coins needed to buy each item, using exact change.

 40¢

 53¢

65¢

78¢

99¢

112

Match Up

DRAW lines to connect coins with the object that can be bought using exact change.

83¢

41¢

95¢

57¢

79¢

Using Coins

Can You Buy It?

COUNT the coins to see if there is enough money to buy each food. CIRCLE **yes** or **no**.

1.     **60¢**   yes   no

2.     **55¢**   yes   no

3.     **98¢**   yes   no

4.     **44¢**   yes   no

5.    **26¢**   yes   no

Who Can Buy It?

CIRCLE the hand of the person who has enough money to buy the robot.

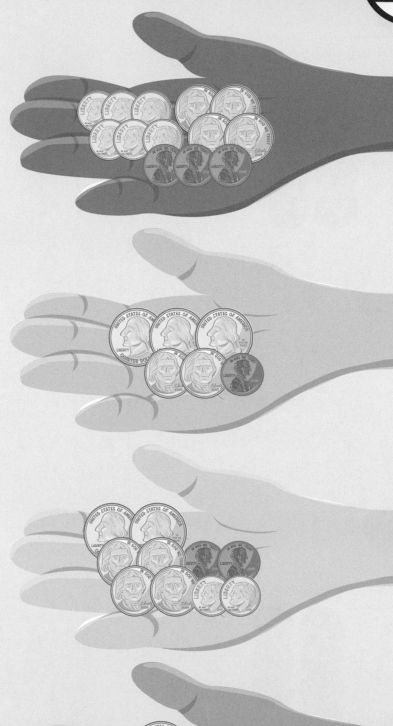

Pay Up

WRITE the value of each coin combination.

1.

2.

3.

4.

5.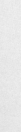

6.

Money Match

CIRCLE the coins to match each price.

12¢

33¢

47¢

51¢

77¢

92¢

Answers

Page 4

Page 5

Page 6
1. 5 + 1 = 6 2. 2 + 3 = 5
3. 6 + 2 = 8 4. 5 + 4 = 9
5. 3 + 7 = 10 6. 4 + 3 = 7

Page 7

Page 8

Page 9
1. 4 + 5 = 9
2. 3 + 2 = 5
3. 1 + 9 = 10
4. 3 + 4 = 7
5. 10 + 0 = 10
6. 7 + 2 = 9

Page 10
1. 3
2. 7
3. 5
4. 6
5. 1
6. 3

Page 11
1. 9   2. 8
3. 5   4. 8
5. 10   6. 3
7. 10   8. 9
9. 10   10. 7
11. 9   12. 7
13. 4   14. 7
15. 7   16. 8

Page 12
1. 3   2. 2
3. 5   4. 2

Page 13
1. 3   2. 4
3. 6   4. 5
5. 2   6. 5

Page 14

Page 15
1. 5
2. 2
3. 4
4. 3
5. 4
6. 4

Page 16
1. 6   2. 2
3. 1   4. 4
5. 1   6. 2
7. 1   8. 5
9. 2   10. 0
11. 6   12. 3
13. 4   14. 1
15. 1   16. 3

Page 17
1. 4 + 5 = 9   2. 6 + 2 = 8
   5 + 4 = 9   2 + 6 = 8
   9 − 4 = 5   8 − 6 = 2
   9 − 5 = 4   8 − 2 = 6
3. 2 + 1 = 3   4. 3 + 4 = 7
   1 + 2 = 3   4 + 3 = 7
   3 − 2 = 1   7 − 3 = 4
   3 − 1 = 2   7 − 4 = 3
5. 1 + 5 = 6   6. 7 + 3 = 10
   5 + 1 = 6   3 + 7 = 10
   6 − 1 = 5   10 − 7 = 3
   6 − 5 = 1   10 − 3 = 7

Page 18
1. 3   2. 5
3. 10   4. 6
5. 2   6. 9
7. 4   8. 1
9. 8

Page 19
1. 9   2. 7
3. 5   4. 10
5. 10   6. 9
7. 8   8. 5
9. 3   10. 0
11. 1   12. 2
13. 2   14. 5
15. 6   16. 1

Page 20
1. 2   2. 1
3. 3   4. 8
5. 5   6. 2
7. 10   8. 8
9. 6   10. 7
11. 9   12. 3

Page 21
1. 4 + 1 = 5   2. 7 + 2 = 9
   1 + 4 = 5   2 + 7 = 9
   5 − 4 = 1   9 − 7 = 2
   5 − 1 = 4   9 − 2 = 7
3. 6 + 4 = 10   4. 5 + 3 = 8
   4 + 6 = 10   3 + 5 = 8
   10 − 6 = 4   8 − 5 = 3
   10 − 4 = 6   8 − 3 = 5
5. 4 + 2 = 6   6. 5 + 2 = 7
   2 + 4 = 6   2 + 5 = 7
   6 − 4 = 2   7 − 5 = 2
   6 − 2 = 4   7 − 2 = 5

Page 23
1. 13   2. 11
3. 12   4. 10

Page 25

Page 26
1. 14   2. 18
3. 12   4. 20
5. 19   6. 19

Page 27
1. 9 + 8 = 17
2. 10 + 6 = 16
3. 7 + 5 = 12
4. 4 + 11 = 15
5. 14 + 5 = 19
6. 8 + 12 = 20

Page 28
1. 5 + 8 = 13
2. 10 + 9 = 19
3. 12 + 5 = 17
4. 7 + 9 = 16
5. 8 + 12 = 20
6. 7 + 5 + 8 = 20

Page 29

Page 30
1. 12   2. 17
3. 6   4. 6
5. 2   6. 8

Page 31
1. 13   2. 17
3. 14   4. 19
5. 19   6. 20
7. 17   8. 14
9. 20   10. 17
11. 12   12. 16
13. 18   14. 16
15. 13   16. 14

Page 32
1. 8   2. 13
3. 7   4. 11

Page 33
1. 5   2. 14
3. 7   4. 5
5. 6   6. 10

Page 34
1. 18 − 13 = 5
2. 16 − 13 = 3
3. 16 − 2 = 14
4. 9 − 2 = 7
5. 18 − 9 = 9
6. 18 − 16 = 2

Page 35
1. 6
2. 9
3. 11
4. 11
5. 0
6. 9

Page 36
1. 7   2. 9
3. 9   4. 10
5. 4   6. 14
7. 16   8. 1
9. 4   10. 14
11. 3   12. 14
13. 2   14. 10
15. 10   16. 6

Page 37

1. 9 + 10 = 19
   10 + 9 = 19
   19 − 9 = 10
   19 − 10 = 9
2. 8 + 3 = 11
   3 + 8 = 11
   11 − 8 = 3
   11 − 3 = 8
3. 5 + 9 = 14
   9 + 5 = 14
   14 − 5 = 9
   14 − 9 = 5
4. 11 + 6 = 17
   6 + 11 = 17
   17 − 11 = 6
   17 − 6 = 11
5. 10 + 8 = 18
   8 + 10 = 18
   18 − 10 = 8
   18 − 8 = 10
6. 14 + 2 = 16
   2 + 14 = 16
   16 − 14 = 2
   16 − 2 = 14

Page 38

1. 14   2. 11
3. 19   4. 15
5. 13   6. 18
7. 12   8. 17
9. 16

Page 39

1. 19   2. 15
3. 20   4. 15
5. 19   6. 17
7. 12   8. 19
9. 6   10. 4
11. 9   12. 17
13. 12   14. 4
15. 9   16. 16

Page 40

1. 8   2. 8
3. 10   4. 9
5. 6   6. 11
7. 13   8. 20
9. 17   10. 18
11. 12   12. 13

Page 41

1. 10 + 3 = 13
   3 + 10 = 13
   13 − 10 = 3
   13 − 3 = 10
2. 13 + 7 = 20
   7 + 13 = 20
   20 − 13 = 7
   20 − 7 = 13
3. 8 + 4 = 12
   4 + 8 = 12
   12 − 8 = 4
   12 − 4 = 8
4. 13 + 6 = 19
   6 + 13 = 19
   19 − 13 = 6
   19 − 6 = 13
5. 11 + 5 = 16
   5 + 11 = 16
   16 − 11 = 5
   16 − 5 = 11
6. 14 + 3 = 17
   3 + 14 = 17
   17 − 14 = 3
   17 − 3 = 14

Page 43

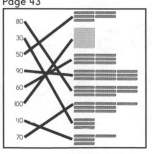

Page 44

1	2	3	4	5	6	7	8	9	10
11	12	13	14	15	16	17	18	19	20
21	22	23	24	25	26	27	28	29	30
31	32	34	35	36	37	38	39	40
41	42	43	44	45	46	47	48	49	50
51	52	53	54	55	56	57	58	59	60
61	62	63	64	65	66	67	68	69	70
71	72	73	74	75	76	77	78	79	80
81	82	83	84	85	86	87	88	89	90
91	92	93	94	95	96	97	98	99	100

Page 45

1	2	3	4	5	6	7	8	9	10
11	12	13	14	15	16	17	18	19	20
21	22	23	24	25	26	27	28	29	30
31	32	33	34	35	36	37	38	39	40
41	42	43	44	45	46	47	48	49	50
51	52	53	54	55	56	57	58	59	60
61	62	63	64	65	66	67	68	69	70
71	72	73	74	75	76	77	78	79	80
81	82	83	84	85	86	87	88	89	90
91	92	93	94	95	96	97	98	99	100

Pages 46–47

1. 45
2. 72
3. 38
4. 67
5. 26
6. 51

Page 48

1. 7 tens, 3 ones, 73
2. 4 tens, 9 ones, 49
3. 5 tens, 7 ones, 57
4. 8 tens, 2 ones, 82
5. 3 tens, 5 ones, 35
6. 6 tens, 6 ones, 66
7. 2 tens, 8 ones, 28
8. 1 ten, 8 ones, 18
9. 9 tens, 1 one, 91
10. 5 tens, 4 ones, 54

Page 49

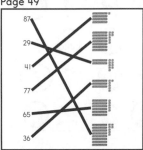

Page 50

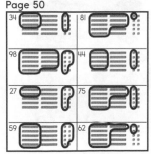

Page 51

1. 2 hundreds, 3 tens, 5 ones, 235
2. 4 hundreds, 1 ten, 9 ones, 419
3. 5 hundreds, 9 tens, 4 ones, 594
4. 3 hundreds, 7 tens, 7 ones, 377

Page 52

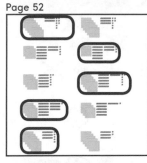

Page 53

1. 912   2. 283
3. 556   4. 769
5. 139   6. 340
7. 428   8. 675
9. 811   10. 506

Page 54

1	2	3	4	5	6	7	8
16	17	18	19	20	21	22	23
26	27	28	29	30	31	32	33
40	41	42	43	44	45	46	47
60	61	62	63	64	65	66	67
82	83	84	85	86	87	88	89
93	94	95	96	97	98	99	100

Page 55

0	1	2	3	4	5	6	7
12	13	14	15	16	17	18	19
31	32	33	34	35	36	37	38
53	54	55	56	57	58	59	60
65	66	67	68	69	70	71	72
76	77	78	79	80	81	82	83

Page 56

2	4	6	8	10	12	14	16
36	38	40	42	44	46	48	50
60	62	64	66	68	70	72	74
5	10	15	20	25	30	35	40
55	60	65	70	75	80	85	90
10	20	30	40	50	60	70	80

Page 57

1	2	3	4	5	6	7	8	9	10
11	12	13	14	15	16	17	18	19	20
21	22	23	24	25	26	27	28	29	30
31	32	33	34	35	36	37	38	39	40
41	42	43	44	45	46	47	48	49	50
51	52	53	54	55	56	57	58	59	60
61	62	63	64	65	66	67	68	69	70
71	72	73	74	75	76	77	78	79	80
81	82	83	84	85	86	87	88	89	90
91	92	93	94	95	96	97	98	99	100

Page 58

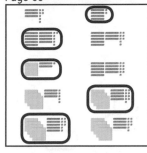

Page 59

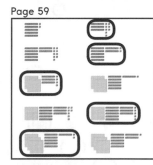

Page 60

1. 79
2. 87
3. 117
4. 240
5. 462

Page 61

1. 32
2. 48
3. 259
4. 298
5. 515

Page 62

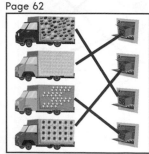

Answers

Page 63
1. 15	2. 68
3. 71	4. 44
5. 263	6. 199
7. 333	8. 920
9. 509	10. 487

Page 64

2	3	4	5	6	7	8	9

53	54	55	56	57	58	59	60

12	11	10	9	8	7	6	5

86	87	88	89	90	91	92	93	94

34	35	36	37	38	39	40	41	42

15	20	25	30	35	40	45	50	55

Page 65
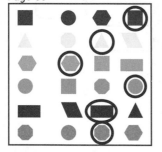

Page 66
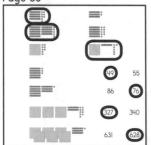

Page 67
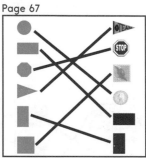

Page 69
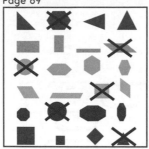

Page 70
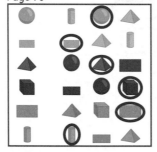

Page 71
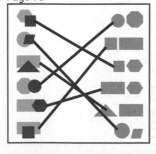

Page 72
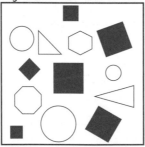

Page 73

Page 74
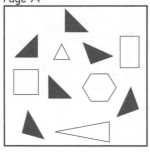

Page 75
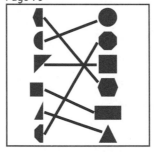

Page 76
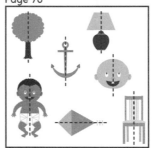

Page 77
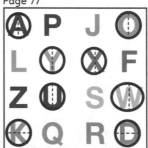

Page 78

Page 79
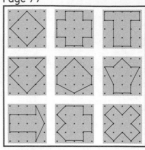

Page 80

Page 81

Page 82
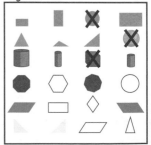

Page 83
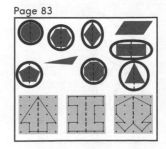

Answers

Page 84
1. 12
2. 10
3. 8
4. 7
5. 6

Page 85
1. 6
2. 4
3. 3
4. 6
5. 2
6. 4
7. 3

Page 86
1. 6
2. 13
3. 4

Page 87
1. 8
2. 4
3. 5

Page 88
1. 6
2. 3
3. 4
4. 2

Page 89
1. 17
2. 13
3. 9
4. 5

Page 90

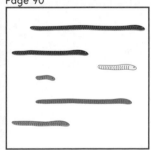

Page 91
Ask someone to check your measurements.

Page 92
1. 6, 15
2. 4, 10

Page 93
1. 2, 5
2. 1, 3
3. 3, 8
4. 4, 10

Page 94
Check:
1. 5
2. 2
3. 6
4. 3

Page 95
Check:
1. 15
2. 9
3. 13
4. 7

Page 96
1. 6
2. 5
3. 3
4. 4
5. 8

Page 97
1. 2
2. 6
3. 2
4. 8

Page 98
1. 9, nine
2. 4, four
3. 3, three
4. 10, ten
5. 1, one
6. 6, six

Page 99

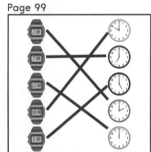

Page 100

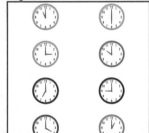

Page 101

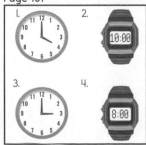

Page 102
1. 5:30
2. 11:30
3. 3:30
4. 9:30
5. 12:30
6. 8:30

Page 103

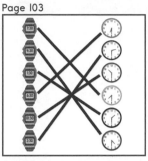

Page 104

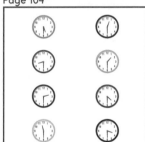

Page 105

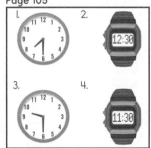

Page 106
1. 1:00
2. 7:30
3. 5:30
4. 3:00
5. 10:30
6. 8:00
7. 9:00
8. 12.30

Page 107

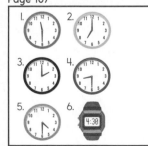

Page 108

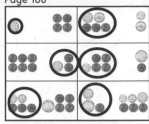

Page 109

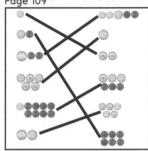

Page 110
1. 9¢
2. 19¢
3. 36¢
4. 98¢
5. 60¢
6. 77¢

Page 111

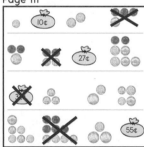

Page 112

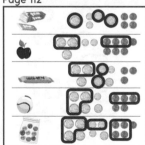

121

Answers

Page 113
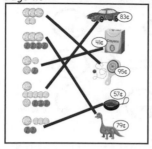

Page 114
1. no
2. yes
3. yes
4. no
5. yes

Page 115
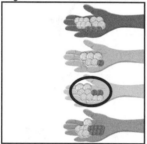

Page 116
1. 28¢
2. 29¢
3. 72¢
4. 90¢
5. 47¢
6. 91¢

Page 117
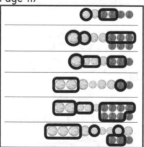